Growing Love's Garden
&
Living Truth Within

by
Robin Wiseman

Copyright © 2002 Robin Wiseman.

All rights reserved. No part of this book may be reproduced or transmitted in any form or by any means, electronic or mechanical, including photocopying, recording, or by information storage and retrieval system, without the written permission of the author, except where permitted by law.

Library of Congress Control Number: 2002110354

ISBN: 1-930648-09-X

First printing, 2002

Cover Art: Ann Rothan
            Watercolor—"Wannabee"
            Print available 16 x 20
            (800)685-1895

Published in conjunction with
Goose River Press
3400 Friendship Road
Waldoboro, Maine 04572
e mail: dbenner@ime.net

Dedication

To my Children, Eddy, Charlotte and Matthew,
who continually inspire me
to walk through love's many doorways.

Acknowledgements

The Guides and Masters who light the way...thank you eternally.
Beloved, I Am climbing the mountain...I offer my love in the oneness.
Mom and Dad and my whole family, thank you for all your love.
Simeon Spillane for exquisite editing style and many hours spent.
Ann Rothan for your gifted artwork and patience.
Debbie Benner at Goose River Press for all your time and effort.
Connie Adkins for all the ways you have lovingly helped me to grow.
Isabelle Tierney, and Eileen McKusick for healing
    insight and heart inspiration.
Yvonne Piette for unconditional love and sharing, and knowledge of
    the Ascension path.
Rose Cote and Paul Chelman for soul beauty inspiration and love.
Paul and Lee-Ann Cournoyer, thank you for the journey of our paths
    joining in growth.

And so many friends, healers, and clients who have extended their love.
Thank you for so many blessings.

Table of Contents

Preface
Prologue
Introduction
Part 1:   **The Gateway to Our Garden**

Chapter One   Willingness and Choice to Know God
Chapter Two   Heart-energy: Truth
Chapter Three   Trust
Chapter Four   Forgiveness

PART II: **The Garden of Springtime—
Planting the Seeds of Love Within**

Chapter Five   Accepting and Loving Ourselves
Chapter Six   Experiencing Soul Beauty

PART III: **Tending and Growing the Garden
in All Seasons**

Chapter Seven   Walking in Balance
Chapter Eight   Growth Spurts

Chapter Nine	Blocks of Resistance
Chapter Ten	Embracing Shadow

PART IV: **Gathering New Bouquets of Love**

Chapter Eleven	Loving for Life: The Mystery of Higher Love
Chapter Twelve	Compassionate Love

PART V: **Ever Blossoming Out in the World**

Chapter Thirteen	Being "Real"
Chapter Fourteen	Fully Creating Outward: Being Love in Walking Action
Chapter Fifteen	Being a Messenger

Preface

This book is the result of a life journey I traveled, at intervals, within a conscious state of the awareness of God. Striving to live the ideas presented here, I came to know that their application is possible for anyone.

In my journey, I experienced a gradual shift in how I viewed the world. Truthfully, I was slow to birth what was inside of me or to turn it into growth because it felt so intense at times. For quite some time, I would continually awaken to more fullness in my life, which seemed to come from many angles—from a broad scope to the minutest details—but I held my own growth at arm's length. Why?

It seemed most challenging to me to accept that this realization of a greater fullness was coming from inside of me. To my surprise, I was growing a sense of my soul's permanence and of feeling its consciousness alive in my impermanent body. And I started to sense that these two levels of being were consciously *blending*. I saw clear visions of their blending.

In the past I had depended on outside experience to form me and to influence my life. Now a slower unfolding was happening—much harder to define, but spilling over with definite gifts and, whether quickly or slowly, heading forward.

The more I have sought the love and guidance of Spirit, the more my life opens to new possibilities, the more opportunities and events play out in my life, helping me to experience shifts in my awareness more consciously and with greater regularity.

Over the course of a year I received spiritual guidance in the form of this writing. Even now, I continue to receive it and to take it down. In working with the writing, I come to understand that I am learning the process by living it, and that this action of living it is my true learning. I've also found that in order to open myself up to new action in my life, I sometimes need to let go of my past definitions and of the feeling that I have to have all the answers.

All through my exploration of self, I have thought about others in the world just like me who may also be experiencing a widening of spiritual perspective. I've tried to imagine how they, and I, might be assisted in integrating this growth. We are *all* challenged with busy and sometimes extremely demanding facets of our lives. As a working mother, I am no exception. Yet it is my hope here that I have grouped chapters in a way that you can follow a clear process—the process of becoming more real to yourself and of living a truly spiritually guided life awake to your soul's essence.

I invite you to share my journey as you further your own. Always I am aware that it is my level of working with guidance that has brought this writing forward and that mine is but *one* perspective. In my life *thus far* I have explored Christianity, Judaism, Sufism, Buddhist and Hindu philosophies—working with Twelve Step Programs, as well as studying the teachings of *A Course in*

Miracles.

    You should know that I respect all paths that lead to God awareness, but feel a special calling to write to address the quest for wholeness coming from a Universal perspective. It is my strong sense that someone from any path, set of practices, or religious discipline could apply aspects of this writing. I have thought many times, "Why do these paths have to be separate? Isn't the ultimate desire of the universe for unity?"

    The word "God," as phrased in this book, refers to the concept of a universal, all loving current that runs through all things. Even the very use of words is a tool to help move us toward a better alignment with that current, which we may come to recognize within ourselves as the principle of "All Is One." The word "Spirit" is used interchangeably here with the word "God." Its illustration in this book is again the energy of *All Is One*.

    The word "Divine" is used to illustrate the integral experience of God's energy unfolding. For ease of interpretation and writing, I refer to God in the masculine pronoun "He," but I in no way intend to ascribe a gender delineation to the Divine Spirit. Please keep this in mind as you read.

    Why do we seek to live a life *full* on the spiritual pathway despite all the determination, willingness, and responsibility that it entails? It is because, as we become more whole in our quest, we connect more fully with the world around us. We help ourselves and others so that the earth may enliven her own potential to heal. The Love that we grow to know assists both we ourselves and everyone around us.

    With all my heart I send forth in love my fondest hope that

you are able to move beyond the words and sense how deeply you are being helped along and guided in your life as you branch out into the vaster, greater capacity of the love of all, *within* all.

This book is a *vibrational* teaching. By that I mean that you will receive its teaching on the level that is right for you, and that if the Divine timing is right for you, you will receive it consciously. It is you who gift these words and messages life within yourself, but even just holding a vibrational teaching will make a positive energetic difference in your life. Read heart-felt words, spiritual words, slowly. Simply let their meaning breathe into you. When words are meant for you they will find their way into your essence. The writing is the laying of a foundation of sorts. May all the words come together to create an opening for sight within you!

Prologue

He brought me the gift wrapped in silk. I stared, removed the ribbon, and said, "You have not brought me the gift."

He stared right through my eyes, into them, and beyond.

"Go then," He said. "Go and find your seeds of heaven wherever you wish."

Then I turned before any more words were spoken. I turned and ran. Oh, how I ran—as fast as my legs were able. I stumbled to the dirt when I felt I could run no longer. Here, the earth seemed to stir with a rumble. Here, I felt I knew that the gift was hidden. I would find it digging beneath the earth's surface. I would uncover the silk covering peering out under layers of dirt. I went about digging, sensing all the while His solid stance very nearby. I felt low and felt somehow one with the ground. Although I did not look up, I felt Him in line with the highest part of the sky, three times as tall as our last meeting, I thought. There seemed a constant buzz and whisper from the trees. I dug until my hands hurt. My fingernails ached and stung. As I sat in rest, a cricket jumped on my knee. It was He, back again...

"So?" He said.

"So!" I slapped my side. Dry dust rose up in the heat of the day.

"I have searched everywhere," I said, you come and you go. You speak of gifts. I can't accept them, or are they buried? You speak of "real," and I don't know what that is, either. I see your blue skies. I feel the moonlit nights. I am always looking to discover, but when do I find?"

I sat in frustrated stillness, waiting motionless in nature. A feeling as strong as wind, but with a warmth, came over me. Though I did not see Him or the cricket now, I heard the words:

"A song that is never ending will forever carry you on its notes, whether you are searching or not. Your belief in truth and in trust moves you to Me and here we birth love. Love is enough to cover the needs of many...and of all. First you will need to hear the song of your own heart, and it is mighty. My gift to you is eternal truth. My gift does not come in silk clothing. It comes in the "real," your readiness to accept it and do as I do..."

My thoughts are suddenly filled with all the senses of being in a garden, but because I do not see it, I am confused...

"Where is this garden?" I ask.

"This garden is us; it is our full music."

"All of us?"

"All of Me and all of you...all of us."

The answers to your prayers were when we met. Don't you know that prayers come in wrappings? You must unfold what keeps you from your own realization of them. The true gift is in the unwrapping or the digging to find, for in that process Divine perfection is found."

"In my case," I said, "I have not recognized it."

"No, you just needed to unwrap a bit further; that is all. Omnipresence is always within you, even when you don't hear it, or think you cannot see a thing."

"Thank you for your kindness," I nod.

"Kindness is a gift we now share, and will continue to

share," He smiles. "And try not to slam any doors as you go along these quicker avenues of learning. Doors are tricky. You will want to close them with reverence, for always there are the energies you cannot catch, you cannot name, but they are with you all the same...extensions of the One truth and gift."

~

Maybe now we will feel a shift in our perspective...
Maybe we will see or sense something differently...
for all of us, the day will come
in Divine order,
when this seeing will begin naturally,
and we will know it is happening within us!
It takes only a small, original sight...
a new "way of seeing,"
to be gifted with knowledge.

Introduction

Many of us are reaching a place in our lives where old concepts just aren't fitting anymore. We process things that we encounter, and at times our faith, religion, or our inner belief system is challenged. In a culture that feeds us with every possible external solution to our dilemmas, it is very difficult to process and honor this shift within. In many ways we feel blessed to have so many resources available to us. Why, then, does it feel so hard to find answers and to rest easy with who we are and where we are going?

There are many ways to break down the questions and theories we could arrive at, but the active questions spurring these theories always seem to remain: the *"What if?"* questions. What if these solutions no longer fit the bill because we are being moved towards a much larger perspective in our thinking? What if, for those of us who have been searching, it was only a matter of time in our lives before we arrived at a new sense of God, and of Spirit, that felt more tangible to us then ever before? What if it was inevitable that we would learn of these deeper truths with certainty before our earth days were over?

Could it be that the wisdom of God is moving us all to seek to know love more fully so that we may better heal ourselves and therefore heal our planet? If so, how can we move forward strongly in love if we don't have a full grasp of what it is within us?

Many teachers of spirituality and the many paths to God believe that, "Truth finds us when we are ready to receive it."

Truth finds each of us differently, but one thing is certain: When truth has somehow softly edged in...past the boundaries of fear...peace is at once created; the sacred space that is graced by love appears. This is because the Voice; the vibration of God is within us. It is heard in the shifting of our thoughts:

- *From questioning to knowing.*
- *From fear to stillness of mind.*
- *From fighting to acceptance.*
- *From the "Little I" to the "I Am."*
- *From human desire for love to the Divine experience of Being that love.*

When Truth and peace want to meet us, we begin to feel there is something more than what we've known, that we are not what we have thought ourselves to be. We all have infinite wisdom within us. By letting go of a fixed way of thinking about our connection to the world and to others, we can begin to experience the depths of our soul's being here.

Ultimately, we do not find fulfillment in this world looking out from a perspective of "I" as our personality, beset with the problems that stem from the conditions of this world:

- The "I" that feels unlovable,
- The "I" that feels misunderstood,
- The "I" who questions my decisions.

The Illusion of Fear

If we see the world as an all-accepting aspect of "I," then we can see ourselves as a piece of it that can be accepted as "I Am." This "I Am" statement means "I Am" part of a greater whole, and I *Am* in motion with it!

When we are locked into all aspects of the personality, we are the "Little I." Who is this? "Little I" is a *fixed* mindset; a way I see the world. The "Little I" looks out and sees a world compartmentalized with judgments and barriers to its expression. The mind projects this outward, and the world, impartial and non-reactive, mirrors it back. The personality level of the mind holds thoughtforms of limitation that block the Spirit's energy flow to us. In other words, we have conditions or illusions in our minds that feed the blockage.

The biggest illusion of all is the fear we have that everything in life has to be a struggle. It feels as if it is a constant struggle because the mind, the "Little I," is trying to run the show. When we find the arms of Spirit, God finding His way to express Himself within us, we start to sense that there is an oceanic flow of right-ordered energy. We make the decision to live in this flow when the other ways of living have become too much of a struggle, or we see many incongruities—when our lives have lost a sense of truth. Indeed, life can feel like a struggle at times, but even when it does we can assist ourselves by seeking a larger perspective.

Another illusion that the mind holds onto is the concept of the world as a fearful, unloving place. We may have worn those glasses for a long time, and it can take time and patience to shift our sight within. To shift perception in this area, we can begin by understanding that what we see in the world is the world mirroring us back to ourselves! This is a simple truth, but it requires our determination to grasp it.

When we are troubled or feel threatened, it is most probable that we have compartments within our minds where these fear-stemming ideas dwell. To desire to grow past this, we must first gain the strength to see the world differently by making a decision to actively seek to know God.

If we seek to see a world of acceptance and universal love, despite the circumstances or the way people are acting, then the world can mirror this wholeness back to us. When we see others living in their compartments of fear, we can love them *without* joining with the fear. When we do this, we help others to move past their fear.

Where there is fear, there is a need for correction of perception. All negative emotions and actions stem from fearful thoughts. When the calling of Spirit finds us, a correction of perception occurs within. As we step up to meet the truth of who we are—expressions of love—we grow towards a much fuller experience of our own lives.

In a way, our lives are an amazing garden made up of all the life experiences that make us who we are. And it is the many facets of love itself that are the food and nourishment that grows the garden of love within us.

As we grow our inner spiritual gardens, we are fueling ourselves by opening inwardly to God, but also seeking to know more of Him in our outward experiences. Our inward acceptance and breathing, receiving of God, encompasses the more feminine aspect of all of us in God awareness. The "seeking to know more of God in outward action" represents the masculine aspect. The receptive and active parts of ourselves *put together* make up our wholeness, our "I Am" presence. The complementary parts of us moving and shifting within create an incredible dance of our soul's energy within body, shining in its awakened states of consciousness.

PART 1

The Gateways to Our Garden

*Staring up the pathway
to the garden's gate,
we can sense that a choice has been made...*

*There is a fuller way
to experience this life.
Its love has many layers...*

*Truth, trust, and forgiveness
are ahead of us on the garden's gateway.*

*We come with the willingness
to see, to sense, and to know
of God more deeply-
to unveil what keeps us
from our realization of Him...*

Chapter One

Willingness and Choice to Know God

When we reach out to God in prayer, or in love, or to find answers, or to be comforted in difficult times, we are connecting with a Force in the universe that is all-loving. It may be helpful to think of God as infinite energy, and we will sense this better as God, through our seeking, reaches to connect with us more fully.

God is All. In some of the ways we have been taught, it is hard to imagine God or Spirit this way. Even when we feel we accept thinking of God this way, we may find ourselves pulled back to our old way of experiencing God as far outside of us. The definitions that we may have held of God live in our mind, where definition and structure, holding on to concept, feel critical to our safety and our innate sense of security.

In our outer life, we set goals for what we want to work towards in our jobs and in our relationships. In the patterns we run, or in things we habitually tell ourselves, we mimic our original love connection patterns learned in early childhood. But running these patterns in adulthood can keep us going in circles, chasing our goals like elusive dreams.

To break down outworn, childhood patterns of behavior in adulthood (both in the way we approach relationships and in the way we approach ourselves), we must consciously choose new ways of seeing and creating. But even after we choose or decide to do things differently, it will take our consistent perseverance and patience to acclimate to new, healthier patterns in our lives. Repetition of that which will maintain our growth and willingness will still be necessary.

On my journey, I began to see that each of us has a distinct personality, one which is an aspect of the mind's expression. The personality is the mind's power point for getting what we want and need in this life. The personality helps us to live comfortably in many ways, but it only moves within a certain energy range up in our minds. Lying on the outskirts of the personality range there is a huge volume of energy that connects us to the awareness of *God as All.* The personality level alone cannot tap into it. There must be a *God-connection* established, and this happens when we choose to seek God more fully than what we have known, read, or been taught.

When we seek more fully, we offer ourselves to God and move past definition. In this place, we make the connection with Him inwardly. For example, in the mind we can say we believe something about God, and this becomes our belief system. Yet to *activate* our belief goes beyond speaking it or defining it. When we start to sense our belief through direct experience, then we know it and it no longer fits the definition of *belief.* Now it is *knowing.* Knowing is found in the heart, not the mind.

When we consciously choose to grow in our awareness, we are walking the spiritual path. Throughout our lives there are invisible doorways through which the energy of Spirit gently calls to us. Choosing to be a seeker and to deepen our awareness of Spirit opens these doorways of direct communication with God. Just as we will come to know our heart center as the receiving point for a fuller love experience of God inwardly, we can also begin to seek God more fully in our outward lives. We can sense this Energy all around us. As we move from one experience to the next, we grow towards a deeper understanding of ourselves.

How does this process happen? First, we make room for this type of awareness by becoming more observant of ourselves and of how we live our lives. Surprisingly, God is found most fully in silence. It is within the spaces of silence that our soul breathes and meets God. Indeed, we are connected to God through our souls, which are the energetic blueprint of God within our finite bodies. In the breathing of silent spaces, Divine Love and soul contact are revealed.

Still, God and the messengers who are a part of God would have us to know that it is not that we are meant to drop everything and become isolated in our lives so that we may come to know more of Spirit. Rather, it is as we go about all the very busy and challenging activities of this life that we are lovingly held by a Constant that we can integrate into our every movement. Through all our experiences, this Constant is ceaselessly moving us to a greater "whole."

Consciousness is an inner manifestation. Our minds are ever busy, so we need to soften our sight and our hearing capacity to sense Spirit. We need to tune into God. How is this done? It takes place through a series of choices.

Our choices start in the deepening of our sight; first, the opening of our eyes to new ways of seeing and then the easing into new ways of being in the world by moving forward fully present to the moment, by surrendering thought of outcome. By our choices, we are erasing thoughts of what we knew to be and breaking new ground each day in moving past what has limited us.

Most everyone today is busy with the details of life and responsibilities. Still, in order to stay with the Truth that creates peace of mind and love action in our lives there is a necessity to make time to "just be." In this action of *just being* we will start to know what we need to do to live with Truth, because living with Truth is the experience of real happiness. Here are some examples to illustrate this principle.

Try admitting for a day that you don't have an answer. Try saying a few, "*I don't knows*," and watch how your body will want to relax. This is a form of surrender, a quieting of the mind. *Not knowing* does not mean you'll be deserted. Not knowing is just letting yourself come up for air in the struggles of this life. In the open air, we tune into God naturally.

Next, imagine your life for a moment existing in a time capsule in the vast ocean of universal experience. In this capsule, you are tuned into the "cosmic radio of God." All your life, the radio gives you messages and inspirations that help you along. This radio of God is on twenty-four hours a day, seven days a week, and it is set to the proper volume. When you take it out in different conditions, it broadcasts with static a lot of the time. Sometimes you cannot hear it come in at all.

Notice how the radio is entirely sensitized to the choices and situations in which you place yourself. The cosmic radio gives you guidance, but you must be the one to train yourself to create a platform for deeper sensing of what it is messaging you. Here are some further examples:

The next time you hear music with vocals, try to move past the voice sounds and hear the instruments in the background.

Stay with the rhythm of the beat. God speaks to us in sound, just as the background instruments do. Behind all our conversations and the busyness of our lives, His Voice is constant. But for the most part, we don't hear the messages because we are used to listening to the vocals, which are the *distractions* in our lives.

Similarly, when something in the environment hints at us over and over again in its loveliness to pay attention to it, God is saying, "Come closer!" If we draw near, we will learn that there is a finer *vibrational* rhythm to the world than we had ever considered.

When you are out walking in the neighborhood you can hear the passing cars. Just for a moment, try to listen to the sound of birds or the sound of the wind behind the car sounds. Nature carries the direct vibration of God because it is part of God's expression of Himself to us. When you are just listening outdoors this way, you are making a direct connection with God. It's such a simple truth that it could pass you by!

A Simple Truth

When you are just listening outdoors,
you are making a direct connection with God.

When you get stuck in fixed ideas about yourself, or others, or your life, you can look at the sky for inspiration. This is an effective form of waking meditation that takes only seconds. The sky is forever shifting and giving forth new, beautiful cloud shapes and colors for you to embrace with each sunset. The shapes and colors provide you with all kinds of messages and encourage you to open your awareness. Even cloudy days speak of the determination you can create in your life.

When you search for God, remember to look and you will see the creation unfolding in all things… Think of an ocean of tropical fish. Where did the colors and patterns in which they run come from? Where did the incredible azure blue ocean originate from? Imagine a sea that, alive and surging under the sun, can move dramatically…beset by powerful, driving winds and rain…the surging waves of a fierce tropical storm. Surely the sun always finds its way through the darkness again, sparkling against the morning glass of a brilliant ocean's surface!

A Deepening Awareness

Through the act of our seeking alone, awareness of God is gifted us. When we first glimpse our awareness deepening, how should we respond? How do we continue to open up even more to God in our lives? Awareness only asks that we reside with it in innocence, cloudlike and confusion free. One moment of suspending our judgment is all that it takes.

If you notice, there is a pattern to the flow of our lives: work, sleep, responsibilities, relationships, quality time. There is also a *Divine* flow pattern in our lives. This is a natural flow of energy that moves us forward to grow and to become all we can become at the rate that is most perfect for each one of us. For this reason, each of our growth rates will differ. This *rate of growth* is sometimes called *Divine order* or flow.

The way to open and allow Divine flow within is by simply

acknowledging that a higher purpose moves through our lives even when we are not aware of it, and by acknowledging that this flow reveals to us truths as we are ready to hear them. Being ready to hear them comes from listening carefully for guidance in whatever form it comes, and from being open to shifts of spiritual growth. Here is an illustration.

Think of a lotus flower…its exquisite beauty growing upward from out of the swampy mud! We may need to put our boots on and wade through some mud in order to clear a pathway for truth in our lives! Once we see a glimpse of truth, are we ready to jump into life and fully experience it in this new light? Are we ready to see color as new each time we encounter it and not just "color that reminds us of something else?"

Life is not a wishing tree with high *wishing branches* growing just out of reach. The wishes are in the trunk of that tree and we also *are* that beautiful tree! Our sight has hidden us from ourselves, but the truth may always be revealed; we just need to seek it out.

Communication Through Gifts

As we open to deepen our awareness, Spirit is able to interplay tangibly in our lives. God is able to gift us a sense of connection through the gifts He gives us of pure sight, synchronicity, and knowing. Most of us think of gift-giving and gift receiving in our lives as special and wonderful. Why? Because it requires special effort and caring on someone's part. We seldom realize that we are gift-giving and receiving with Spirit all the time in all the ways of learning, knowledge, and blessings that come into our lives. Likewise, we may give back to God by saying, "thank you," and by feeling true gratitude for His gifts. When we share our gratitude with others and by living our lives with devotion we begin to treat what we are given by God with reverence.

Pure Sight

Pure sight is an original gift from God. This sight is the light of God. Seen on any level, it will cast a different glow on everything. It is a form of blessing. Doubtless, things will shift in sight, sense, and feeling when we are blessed with this sight. Pure sight will embody an innocence that feels new—like the vision of a shiny new penny, a fuzzy baby chick, or a red rosebud just before its petals unfold!

In the moment that pure sight touches our consciousness, we are looking at the all-new in a space of purity. If we let it in, we will be shown the evidence of love to our eyesight more deeply than we have known. The sight comes from our hearts own resonance to God. Moments of seeing are a pathway to more blessing.

Synchronicity

The gift of synchronicity from Spirit happens in awareness when our lives seem to become easier with a better flow. We will sense coincidences of being at the right place at the right time, getting a phone call from a friend just as we pick up the phone to call them, unexpected happy surprises. These are all ways God lets us know we've allowed our pathway of seeking to become wider. Synchronicity offers us proof that a right-ordered flow is moving through our lives to help us keep its expression free and clear. When we find ourselves with unexpected but welcome smiles on our faces, when we can know Higher forces are at work for the better in our lives.

Knowing

When we receive the gift of knowing from God, our hearts are touched and our sense of separation from others begins to dissolve. It may happen gradually, or in many small but marked instances. No one is able to describe these moments fully, because they are too exquisite for words to really capture...so we continue to grow at just being. Then, when the second or moment of realization arrives, we can give inward thanks to God. Consider the following familiar experience.

You have a sudden inspiration that a sign has been given to you....a warm rush or chill that washes over you, but it is difficult to define easily. At times like these, it's important not to let the awareness go, because it can slip through your consciousness like the blink of an eye. Write the experience down or, better yet, let heaven know that you felt it by giving full thanks. That way your heart will remain open to receive more knowing in the future. Our tendency is to not stay with the knowings of our hearts. It's as if we don't feel worthy of such completeness within ourselves.

The next time you think of something you have a strong feeling or knowing about, ask yourself why you might hold the feeling at bay, as if it cannot be yours. Now back up and observe.

Deep feelings of the heart resonate God-energy. Yet that which is of God cannot be owned because it is everywhere. It is beyond the slightest or fastest vibration you could imagine…and it is part of us. Why? Because we are all part of a greater whole.

When the gift of knowing touches awareness, it produces a love that is often felt with sweetness in the fullness of our hearts. This is a sweetness that is not induced by a substance or situation outside ourselves. It is a God-awareness that we breathe in by our desire to let ourselves be ourselves.

Truly, there are many doors in heaven—in the upper realms—each with gifts behind them. We do not have to go to heaven to receive the gifts; we only need to draw the light of heaven through these doorways by calling to it with our love for life and our seeking through that love.

The Existence of Guides

There are higher dimensions of energy just beyond our level of existence, which function at a more rapid energy frequency. We may know of these realms but have a hard time integrating our belief in their reality because we cannot always see this higher vibration with our open eyes. Yet perceiving higher dimensions is possible. How?

The beginning of the sight of them looks like seeing tiny moving particles in the air. The air will have a transparent, effervescent movement to it. What you are seeing here is pure energy. Dashes of light or vivid color, especially on the edge of sleep, are also signs of energy and guidance dwelling close by.

In our mind's eye (located in the center of our foreheads, the brow, in long concentration or meditation with an open heart), it is much easier to see further into the upper dimensions. Most people who have had near-death experiences describe these dimensions vividly and speak of a "tunnel" that leads through them to the light of total oneness with God.

There are guides and Masters around each of us- beyond that which we are able to physically touch in this dimension. Guides are there to help us through our learning in this life. Masters, such as Jesus or Buddha, walked the earth at one time as great teachers of love and light. As Ascended Beings, they are able to continuously offer eternal wisdom, unconditional love and support from the upper realms. Guides may be closest to this physical dimension, as in those who assist with the balancing of the earth, elemental Beings, or those of the *fairy realm* as they are sometimes called.

A Master or guide will not interfere with our actions in this life in any way. They are an extension of the light shining upon us and within us. They offer us pure love...that we may better know of all we are.

Communication or assistance from Masters and guides is entirely dependent on our ability to let go of definition. We can only communicate or sense their guidance through the open spaces within our hearts and minds. Thus, in our own need to hang on to what's known, we are the only stoppage to the pathway through to knowing more of what we believe or what we define ourselves to be.

There are many ways that we receive awareness of guidance. Some of us are clairvoyant; we see, to varying degrees, through the realms. To be clairsentient means to "sense" or feel guidance through the body. *Clairaudience* is the ability to hear guidance. Guides communicate through the veils in the way that is right for each person. No one way is stronger or more attuned than another, but sometimes we will posess more than one ability to know guidance.

There are two types of Divine messaging that we receive from spirit. The first is guidance through any of the senses noted above. This form of messaging feels direct and can help us with decisions or choices in our lives, or to simply have a deep feeling that support or assistance is close by. As we live more focused in the moment, we are opening to this messaging from the upper realms.

A Simple Truth

*We stabilize in the energies of balance
and life's purpose;
what it truly means for us to be alive, when we live
the instructions that are given to us.*

In sensing the guidance of Spirit, you will often be given directions, great and small. If you don't block them out, the "directions" automatically work with you to keep your life simple so that you can ride life's natural energy waves instead of thoughts of fear that can pull you off balance.

This Divine communication is around you and will find you naturally in your process of seeking. All you must do is *will* to make peace with your natural energy level each day. Keep asking and staying open to guidance, and do not fall prey to the pulling and pushing of this life. If you do get caught up in the extremes, realize that *that* level will be drawn to you, so it will feel harder to rise above problems.

There is no limit to questions we can ask in guidance of Spirit. We can release the questions knowing that the release returns Divine messaging back to us. A question might look like, *"If I can't see the pathway in front of me, where am I supposed to be headed?"* or, *"Why isn't this situation working out the way I had hoped it would, and how can I better grow through it?"*

The second form of Divine messaging is an actual energetic shift in our consciousness that moves us into a fuller sense of our spirituality. The Divine speaking to you this way is a direct transmission of energy to you. You can picture these messages as a glow of God's care illumined from within you, or a beautiful rainbow light shower coming down all around you. It is meant to gently awaken you further.

When we receive this energetic form of Divine messaging we are evolving more quickly spiritually to the awareness of our soul's light. It is a truth that finds its way into our whole selves before we are even fully aware of how it entered. These messages are very difficult for the linear mind to process. Mind thoughts stay in the mind. Divine "thoughts" circulate throughout the body at a cellular level, bringing in light. For this reason, we may feel the pace or activities of our lives slow down naturally at the edge of such a shift. Then we are more open to receive.

Divine messages of both kinds will come into your life as many times as necessary before you hear them. *You* are the strength behind any Divine message because you make yourself open to receive it. When your heart is kept open, then it can be alive within you vibrationally. But how do you respond to Divine messaging?

First, you absorb the truth of the message; then you have the choice to live the truth in right action in your life. It is important to let the whole self gradually grasp a "higher mind" concept. The time it takes to "get it" may seem very slow, so we can do ourselves a favor by recognizing that there is no timer waiting to go off!

We are so hard on ourselves when light energy wants to come and dance with us! Any thought of confusion is enough to blind our sight of awareness. The message is so faint to us, only because we are not accustomed to it. It is not something we have known in our minds. If we were trained by television to absorb light in messages, then this form of messaging would not seem so out of place to us. But this communication's frequency is far above a radio or television wave.

What we usually see in front of us is our own comfort zone. When we fine-tune our awareness in moment-by-moment living, we will catch the Divine messages that are just waiting to grace us. The veils of separation lift as we grow. The more we receive these messages, the more we shift into deeper awareness of love and light.

Truly, to be one who seeks to know God more fully through all of the ways that experiences come before us is to be a pioneer in this life. It is to be of assistance in opening doorways for mankind…

Angels Among Us

Angels carry the awareness of our happiness all through the hands of time. They are for us, offering to save us from the illusions that make us feel so incomplete. Still, angels will not plead with or demand anything from us because they do not interfere with the choices we make. They carry Divine messaging on their wings, which is meant for our ears alone—when we can tune in on high to hear them. We might hear them as tones in our ears, as the sound of bells, or sometimes as music. Our higher selves, an aspect of our soul-knowing, are very connected to angelic assistance. Without even knowing that we've received it, we receive help from the angels all the time! Angels assist us most readily in dreamtime while we sleep.

A Simple Truth

*If you can be at peace right now
believing that your life is
ordering itself out perfectly,
then you can start to sense angelic
presence in your life. It is that simple.*

Angels operate in our lives at a level of deep knowing that because we are created in the image of God we are perfect love. This is how they reach us. They experience us as the same perfect love that they are. From their perspective, the sabotage we throw out into our lives simply is not there. When they "zoom" in to assist us, it is because a glitch to the pathway of our love connection stands out dramatically, like a black ink spot on a white sheet. A cry is heard instantaneously in the upper realms, where crying is not part of natural ordering.

Although one guardian will come to your side, there are many others beside that one. Since space is not a factor for them, they may crowd a room without measure. They are able to work with light rays when we dream to illuminate remembrance points for our conscious minds. They work with light at the threshold of death to illuminate our way home.

To bring your angels closer to your awareness, all it takes is the awakening of an opening in your mind and heart. You can think of your Guardian Angels as those loving Beings who had been your best friends before you came into this life.

Angels serve in archways that might be called *gateposts*. These are "spots" of brightly lit illumination that shower us with a deep recognition and appreciation of God within. The love of God knows absolute perfection, but something in the translation of ourselves into the physical world caused in us a forgetfulness of this fact. Angelic presence serves to remind us of it.

Thinking of an angel as a solid, winged human is romantic and impacting for us, but the angels would remind us that they are "light as the breath" and to really be in touch with them is to sense them as ethereal and illuminated, like sparkles on the breeze…just barely turning to form. They remind us that although they come into our space ethereally, they have strength and flexibility, supporting themselves through the many densities they must sometimes wear. They offer to us that in a glass or window reflection, or out of the corner of our eyes, they might appear as a flash of light. It depends only on how the linear mind would need to grasp it. Certainly they *could* manifest in a winged form.

One of the angels' central teachings is that of eternity. Like the light that forms the "halos" on their heads, the circle is one of their primary symbols, teaching of "no beginning and no end." The light shines onward to infinity. It is the one light of direct source. It does not shift in intensity. When we see it, we interpret it this way because at times there is a message in the light that affects the way it comes to us.

Angels were not once human; they are actually pre-human, meaning that when Divine order presents itself they are able to assume human form and be of service. There is an aspect; a process of forgetting that they too, like ourselves, must go through to assume physical form, and they must undo the forgetting, as a human being would. Yet their awareness may speed up dramatically in conjunction with their work because of the fact that they are running outside of a linear time format.

Spirit guidance and the angels of God, in whatever voice or essence presents itself in our lives, are there with complete support. It is we who must choose in this life to be the seekers, to be people who seek to know God more fully. Because guidance asks us to become all we are capable of being, we have to desire this in our lives most consciously and deeply.

*The heart gifts the deepest
of knowing...
It is a passageway not traveled
by walking feet.*

*I cannot go to approach
love that is already there.
It finds me in my awareness and then I know
because my cup runs over.
I cannot question,
but I can witness it.
I cannot own it,
But I can flow with it.*

*Now I am sustained by the light within me.
Into every cell of my body
It feeds me with wisdom,
It feeds me with strength,
It fuels me with the sustenance and beauty
of love.*

Chapter Two

Heart-Energy: Truth

In consciousness there are instructions for us at the gateways of deeper knowing. These gateways are truth, trust, and forgiveness. They are the pathways to Higher Love and wisdom. The energy of God makes its fullest connection to us at the heart's center in presenting us with the truth of who we are. Knowing truth is more of a sensing than a mental understanding. Bear this in mind as you read this chapter, which may seem a bit hazy to your untrained mind.

Heart energy feels elusive to us because truth messages grace the heart in love vibration rather than words. The heart receives and emanates this love vibration because it is the center of love within our bodies. To hear the heart as truth we move into listening from a place of innocence. Our seeking begins and ends with the foundation in our hearts and proceeds, largely dependent on how *we open* to receive God from this foundation.

The truest sense of home is within your heart. There are ways to make yourself externally content in this world, but the degree to which you come home to the spaces of love in your heart is the degree to which you are present to others and the degree to which you show up for life fully.

The truth in the heart is God's instruction to us that we are love, and that the love we are is our soul's representation here in our bodies. It is a seed or spark that is eternally planted within our hearts. This is just beyond a closed door that holds us from it. Reaching out to God and getting still opens the door.

A Simple Truth

*The truth in your heart is that you are love.
Your soul is here
within the bodies impermanence so that you
can discover that love consciously.*

The heart expands in love in the rhythm of "towards life," not of "turning away" from it. Thus, at any given moment of the day we are moving either away from the present moment in fear or opening toward it in love. Our hearts are the most beautiful of flower blossoms, and the many silken petals within us open outward toward life or gently fold inward in shielding, depending on the circumstances in which we place ourselves.

How present are you at any given moment? In being fully present, your heart recognizes its love and you are home. When heart-energy lands in awareness, all feels right. We feel we don't have to move or change anything, so we can be fully present. This evokes a tremendous sense of relief. All is well.

The sense of "all is well" is our inkling from God that He is not as elusive as we may have sensed. When this moment finds us, we know that nothing needs to be changed. We are being ourselves within the full power of the moment. Here there is centering. Here there is a sense of *home base* deep within that no outward situation can affect.

When we have gone through difficulties and have doubted ourselves, how can we be sure we'll hear when we ask the question, "What is the truth of my heart, and how do I recognize it?" Sometimes we have to sit with the question for a time, not having any sense of the answer. The answer comes to us when we are truly ready to hear truth, and not before, and most often we do not hear it from another, but from our own heart.

Sometimes to receive a truth we need to be entirely empty-handed. This is why, at times, we are first found by God in times of great sorrow or difficulty. Through a major shift in our lives, a big event or a loss, a strong connection made with another person, a spiritual awakening, or a relationship ending or beginning, we often find a contact point with truth.

Moreover, we will know truth, if we are willingly seeking it, to the exact level that it is right for us. This truth is simple knowing, so simple that it is difficult to follow here in our lives on earth, because truth provides immediate access to the very center of who we are.

A Simple Truth

*Being ready to hear means inviting your
heart-energy to shine.
To hear, you begin to open ever so slightly
toward being a part
of love's expression through willingness.*

To seek truth means being ready to experience it, prepared to see your essence in light and in love. We grow more towards the realization of this love throughout our lives. It is what we do with this truth that shapes our destinies. Perhaps God would tell us that there is no right or wrong path, no right or wrong decision that we could make. It is all learning. It is the degree of spiritual truth that we allow into ourselves that creates the threshold that we choose to live our lives before, and this is completely our choice. Sometimes the path of right action appears to us in stages, and sometimes there seems to be no pattern at all.

As we meet the truth of the love that we are, we start to come out of a small shell into a larger way of seeing. The small shell had represented a shielding we felt we needed to protect ourselves from hurt and pain. But if love is with us at all times, emanating from our hearts, then we can realize that the shielding we put there serves no purpose to the newfound awareness because there is no stronger truth than this love. As we lift the shell off by listening in our hearts and staying with Truth or our inner voice, we find that we can love more fully.

The language the heart speaks is honoring this truth of love and walking in the natural rhythm of this life in truth. The heart breathes the energy of oneness of Spirit, no matter what all the complications the mind places before it may be. The heart kept open in willingness to stay present to the moment fuels us with energy to live fully in this life.

Are we willing to meet the foundation in our hearts, and are we open there to receive this love? What in the world does *that* *l*ook like? Is it possible to build this? To seek and to know Truth is to connect with a trusting that it is possible. Here is an exercise that may help you:

In order to initially receive love in the heart, still your mind and rest with the truth that first and foremost, you are a representation of love. You are love. In the place of love inside you there is innocence. This innocence was your original reception of love, before your mind grew as you grew up. In the innocence of your childlike heart there is only a seeking of love and a wanting to be heard.

In the stillness of a quiet place, go deep into your mind. Find the center of your innocent child-self, and ask it what it seeks. Ask, "What do you need?" This becomes the doorway to the heart, because its answers are only found in complete innocence. Do not judge what you hear in any way. These truths are the seeds of who you truly are, sprouting outward so that you can know yourself more fully.

On an ongoing basis, slow yourself down and become observant. Start to listen to yourself and to what is taking place in your life…without judging yourself. Don't be discouraged. You must truly listen, many times. As you listen, remind yourself of the love that you are, beyond all the voices. This reinforces the strength of love within you.

The Voice of Innocence

As we work with the Voice of Innocence within we are remolding our sense of ourselves. We are becoming the adult of today—with an awareness of the original innocence of the child within our heart. We are building a sacred essence, an ethereal light structure in our hearts. The childlike foundation in our hearts says that we are love, and this love breathes in our hearts.

Because we have been used to functioning in this world primarily from the mental spaces of the mind, the first sounds of heart-energy being heard in us will feel strange and new, and our awareness may initially feel fleeting. But as we cultivate self-love, truth will reside with us as a constant. Heart-energy speaks in vibration more than in words, and feelings of the heart seem only fleeting because we aren't used to them. They follow a purer wavelength than all the intense thoughts of our minds.

Although heart's energy is not that of logic, we can be fully present to the truth of love and still pay attention to the mind. Through being observant without judging, and through letting Spirit guide to right action in the things that come up, we let our thoughts flow forth.

To live heart-energy to its full potential, a desire for control cannot be present. If we are always looking for life to be "just so," or forcing things to become the way we want the future to be, we won't make heart-energy fully at home in our hearts. This is the most difficult step for many of us because we fear change and loss of control. Yet when we give up a need to control, we find that we are not lost but found and discover the innocence within.

We step up to meet heart-energy when we find our ability to surrender to all of life's conditions and step into a place of moving *with* life rather than of acting or reacting to it. It is here that we experience grace…

Grace finds its way to us. The touching of heart-energy doesn't put brakes on the thoughts of the mind; it simply eases the mind and allows it to come up for some fresh air. In these moments, the whole self is rejuvenated.

Warm feelings of love run in patterns and rhythms. The rhythm is much larger than our mind's ability to comprehend, so the best way to *be with* feelings more deeply is just to flow with them.

The Heart's Shielding

The heart has shielding, but nothing like the walls of the mind, which often want to determine exactly what will be. While the mind blocks mentally, the heart shields itself by fending off emotions based on fear and separation. When we hold fear, the heart's energy becomes blocked. When the heart-shielding comes off through opening energetically, emotion may be expressed through deep grief, tears, and sobs—all the ways the heart has to work to be held back from imaginary separation. Here, the heart grieves for the lost sense of itself—at last releasing its pangs of fear. The heart energetically cries out in the release, "I want to be all that I Am within you!"

The deeper the heart's resonance to love, the more shielding it would put forth if the mind registered hurt on an emotional level. Within the truth seeker, the heart, wanting a complete expression of love, will make clear what is not being expressed or honored in our lives.

A Simple Truth

When you can recognize resistance to truth, say,
"I no longer want to shield,"
then feel yourself being carried by a greater current of
sustenance and becoming partner to the feelings that

come up for you. Steer your way through these feelings, knowing you are opening up to more self-care in your life.

We may have been used to big *hellos* and intense *goodbyes* with our feelings, to doors flung open suddenly or slammed very quickly shut. Heart-energy cannot be confined to the fears in our minds that wish to control emotion. Heart-energy simply exists in unflinching, constant flow beneath the personal dramas we create around feeling. Try the following exercise.

To experience deeply touching heart-energy, sit quietly in a favorite spot. Slowly relax your body, your neck, your shoulders…any body part in which you feel tension. Breathe into your heart center, your chest. Connect with the rising and falling of your breath…expansion and contraction. Slowly open your mind. Release your thoughts by focusing inwardly on the air in the room. See it in your mind's eye as completely filled with warm, brightly lit energy. It is colorful, it is sustaining, and it is pure love.

Now place a hand gently onto your heart-center. As you breathe in deeply, imagine you are drawing in this love energy with each incoming breath. It is an inexhaustible resource being offered to you. Feel it connect with your heart and, with each breath, feel it spread throughout your body. Slowly feel its warmth satiate your senses. Let yourself bask in its glow. Feel this radiance within. This is the radiance of God's love, and it is an integral part of you in every way. It is unconditional, whole, and safe. Breathe it in with awareness as often as you are able…

Heart-energy moves out only from truth and love. It speaks

the language of honoring the truth of who we are. When we stay in heart-energy, we walk the rhythms of this life in truth. When we ride that wavelength, we are fully alive and have opened the channels to Spirit, to God.

*Trust is the action
of walking through.
It is the precise action
of anchoring the love
that you are,
thus being able to
extend it to others...
from within...
going the distance in action,
and covering love's ground.*

*This is sacred ground that
we cannot know,
except as we continually
pass through it.*

Chapter Three

Trust

When we are at the edge of taking new ground, experiencing deeper self-love, and seeking a deeper realization of God in our lives, trust is presented to us as a means to help us get through the shifts we feel within. Trust is supreme assistance from the upper realms. It is the second gateway to knowing love's garden, which grows within us. It is an ever-present energy, and it is graced to us as we *walk it* in our actions, surrendering all thought of outcome to God.

After we move into the deeper spaces of exploration within ourselves, we may still feel we have come up empty-handed in understanding. When we can't understand mentally, there is a hesitancy, many times, to move forward. But if we continue to hang on to hesitation in our minds, it remains hard to understand the concept of Divine love as part of who we are. We may also meet with resistance of various kinds in our minds.

As heart-energy continually moves to create more happiness and joy in our lives while we seek for it in willingness, we learn to be with this new flow. Trust is the central tool that creates knowing and confidence from the action of walking it in our lives. But what does it really mean to trust?

Trust is not found exclusively in the mind. It is the action of moving across a living bridge—from our minds through to our hearts. We are moving from what we have held in personal definition into the presence of God in an experience of oneness. Heart-centered energy weaves all throughout trust, fortifying us to move past the edges of what we know toward the love connection within us. When we choose to trust, we step through to new ground. We do this by living *the love that we are* in walking action, even when we can't know or define what is in front of us.

Trust is a process. It is not previewed or experienced ahead of time, nor can we just request it and wait passively for it to come. As we walk in trust, we are shown trust. Only then do we experience a passage into true security. The result is peace and happiness in the moment, or constancy and a deeper sense of our strength. But where does trust come from?

God presents us with trust as a tool when we are the closest to knowing Him. *Knowing* is an absolute thing, and trust must be the absolute action that partners with it. It may help you to think of trust like this: The rain falls and cleanses, the wind blows and shifts, the sun shines and clears our thinking, and we *begin to begin* again. The motion of all of creation, constantly renewing, is the energy of God. Trust allows us to walk in harmony with this motion, but it must be allowed for. If we allow for trust in our lives, Spirit will show us how to move through this life with our sense of spiritual awareness intact.

Our strength, at its fullest, is our ability to be present in a finite physical body and to know at a cellular level the "Love of All," through our "I Am" presence. The hands of Spirit hold all that we need to walk in trust, beyond the trappings of our minds, which in their limitation do not have the capacity to assimilate this concept.

We can bless our mind inwardly for the incredible capacities that it does have—its logic and reason—but with mind only we can go no farther... As we walk in trust, we are being shown a new way *to be* in this love, and all we are being asked to do is to move forward in moment to moment, trust-filled action, as aware as we can be.

As we walk through life, our physical bodies are our truest friends. We have these bodies to experience all of life on earth, the richness of duality. But in the present day the concept of duality, light and darkness, is shifting now to move towards a greater whole of the experience of oneness. Through our conscious connection to God we can come to know our soul's experience of oneness even in our physical body. This manifests as the expression of love whenever we let it through. Love cannot judge; it simply flows as love and offers kindness and compassion wherever it reaches. When we acknowledge this flow consciously, we may feel new feelings that we have a hard time placing or sense changes and choices we need to make. Many times we will feel intense resistance. That is because Divine flow will want to move you past the blocks in your life that hold it away.

Again, what is trust? Trust is knowing that I stand on the edge of recognizing who I Am in the light of God and that my feet are moving. It is not me moving my feet, and yet it is the *all of me*. In my journey, I stopped and dropped the questions of why I felt called forward. I just started to walk. The intensity of the call or its exact definition I did not know ahead of time, but I deeply acknowledged it as part of a greater flow—emanating from my heart in search of connection to God.

You may experience this actual transformation to a freer experience of who you are in this life and feel like you are standing at the edge of something greater, yet not know how to move into it. It may feel to you as if the pieces to the puzzle of how you were living don't fit anymore. You may see one small clue or many. Still, if you are growing, you are facing the unknown... and you will feel the calling to go forward, even through your resistance.

At times like these Spirit will offer us a bridge of trust—of undeniable, unwavering support—a stronghold or a Constant to help us move forward through the challenges, but we must take the action to move forward, surrendering our fears to God. By this action, we are birthing new levels of ourselves in new awarenesses never before known to us.

A Bridge of Trust

What would a bridge of trust look like? A bridge often symbolizes assistance with self-growth and transformation. It is the structure, whether visible to the naked eye or not, that moves us from one place in our lives to another. It is strong and its support is unwavering.

A bridge rarely gives up its form in the merciless flights of fancy thrown at it from storm surges or high winds. Some bridges were built for high speed trains shooting across them in the night, some for hikers gingerly moving between one precarious rock cliff to another.

What would your bridge of assistance to trust look like in your mind's eye? Does it feel really intense and challenging, or wide and yielding to any way in which *you* *w*ould choose to cross it?

The bridge might tell us to welcome the steep height as a challenge that would reveal our strength. The bridge might tell us to not focus on the height, but to focus steadfastly on each step we take to cross it, for each step is a movement of trust, and courage and trust undeniably feed self-love.

Courage is a space that we are given to move us in alignment with a deeper purpose. It is a tool to align us with trust. Courage is found when we are faced with a trial and feel there is no way but through it. Spirit would have us to know that there is a deeper current beneath courage, a deeper sight that is gifted. It is our own expansion, for when we've begun walking in courage and trust, we can recognize that we have many more expressions within us than we've ever even dreamed. Try the following exercise.

Picture your bridge again. Let it speak to you of your courage and clarity of mind. Look at the strength of its structure. Feel your faith in trust. Walk your dreams by the hand across this bridge—made up of all the love and support the heavens can supply. It is made up of all the components you've built to get you exactly to where you are now. All you need to do is feel the trust and walk across it. Sometimes at the other side of the bridge you will see what you are wanting to move through. The bridge will show you that you can go the distance and gain deeper perspective. You may question the details of how you've arrived here. You question… now you are being guided to stop the questioning. Release your fear in trust and innocence…

As we get a sense of the surroundings at the edge of our bridge, we may also look back in tender moments and question the past. Moving to trust is slow, and may involve returning to the healing work within ourselves. This is because trust is the action of allowing ourselves to anchor to our hearts in deep love.

When we can stay with Trust in this life, especially during difficulties, we assist others to trust more fully by our example. We mirror to each other what needs to be healed between us. Trust is committing to go the distance of covering love's vast ground…sacred ground that we only experience as we walk through it. God wants to show each and every one of us that we are created in His image, which is pure love.

Our action of trusting lets God know we believe in the love that is. Maybe we can't see it, but when we trust, we bridge the gap. The fuel in our lives that Trust creates is true sustenance. As we walk, sometimes in silence, we will sense the answers that we need to live day by day. The answers will come as we are living trustfully.

When we are formulating in our minds, we feel we must figure everything out. We bring stress and worry upon ourselves. In trust, we can stop trying so hard all the time to figure every detail out, as it uses up so much of our energy. Love energy has an intelligence—just as logic does, but it is from the larger supply of God-energy, the same energy we are made from. When we can live life in awareness of this Divine energy current, the answers will find us. As we are living, we will be shown right action. Our hearts will verify the right actions to us; decisions will feel right at a centered level.

One thing is certain: God messages that as you cross your first bridge in trust, you will see other bridges before you in the distance—each one unique and beautiful with the light of wisdom and knowledge. With each trusting choice you make, you can know more deeply that you are fully supported. And the path across your bridges will be wide or narrow depending on each unique life situation you encounter.

Trust is a stronghold for us, illumined with Spirit's love, which moves us to express ourselves in fuller love for ourselves and for all humanity. We look for definition because we cannot allow ourselves to think how things could be different. The action of trust establishes a new way of seeing. As we continue to affirm God as a Presence in our lives and take action in trust, the awareness of Spirit's sustaining love is kept alive in our hearts and souls, and we know ourselves more deeply in the inner strength we have gained.

*Who was I
to think that I had
this huge map of life
all figured out?
What stresses I've brought
on myself...
for the structures I put
myself up against
were too small.
Whose race am I running?
What is this Life asking me to be?
How can any of us be fully all that?*

*Let me be found
in the spaces of let go.
Let me be found
in the spaces of breathe.*

*The past is a rich, silken tapestry
that I spun to grow.
The future is a dream I've yet to travel.*

*I am fullest in the here and now,
so I choose now
to accept,
to forgive,
to be just who I am.*

Chapter Four

Forgiveness

The deepest part of our souls, in energy that we can recover and that is rightfully ours, is complete forgiveness of ourselves on all levels for all that we are, for who we *are not,* and for where we have been in our lives up to this moment. Forgiveness is an action of full release graced to ourselves and to others.

Being willing to seek truth—beyond excuses and no matter what—will bring us face to face with an awareness of forgiveness. The weaving of forgiveness is the work of angels, showing us that every experience brought us closer to the truth of our soul as love.

True forgiveness spans across all time and space because it declares we are all in the sacred process of moving toward our Divinity. Our rates of moving forward may seem to differ, but in actuality they do not. It is only the shifting in the mantle of what holds us from ourselves in true expression that is subject to time.

When you have reached the point of wanting to make positive changes in your life, you are staring into the eyes of forgiveness, no matter how thick the lens may seem. To make truly permanent shifts in your life, you will need to let go of attachment to the past, as well as to the future. Changing thoughts that bind you to the past or future is a decision, and the process is fueled by the very decision you're asked to make.

The past is only a memory, and while memories can be incredibly rich, they do not actually carry energy to fuel our lives in the present. The energy of God is in a constant state of creation and renewal. When we can look at our lives, for a moment, from a broad perspective and forgive ourselves for what we saw as our past mistakes and shortcomings, we free our energy to dwell in the present—and action transmits from Spirit!

Events from the past may have left us in a place of judgment and unwillingness to fully forgive ourselves or others. To surrender completely, we need to believe that we are worth our own best effort. Spirit cannot *gift* in new energy to help us if we cannot let go of the past… But what will it take to do so?

The ability to let go of unforgiveness requires only that you ask Spirit for it: "I ask for acceptance of what and where I Am right now, and I forgive myself and/or others for past actions and reactions." That is all. A state of willingness to release in the now gives up our struggle in the mind. Then doorways for positive that had always been available to us can present themselves with simplicity, serenity, and happiness.

Many of us want to see positive changes occur in our lives, but we project our desire into the future, waiting for some far off event on the horizon to target towards, reach, and then make the shift. Why wait for that event in the future? The full power to create change is available to you in the now; you need only surrender to its strength.

Forgiveness: the Healing Flow

Letting go of what we think our future should look like takes the willingness to move through fear. Sometimes fear will come up for us as a huge bubble—many troubling thoughts inflating themselves at once—and it needs to be lifted away.

We get upset about mistakes we feel we have made in the past, and we cling to the negative memory of them, which binds us from surrendering to our future. We are fearful that we may repeat our former difficulties or suffering, so we try to mold a future pathway to our desires. Still, our fears, especially the fear of repeating patterns from the past, are all too often projected forward.

Unforgiveness weaves through all other emotions, obstructing their path. Meeting unforgiveness head on takes us out of the mind sway between past and future tenses. The act of forgiving ourselves is the act of releasing what we feel our faults to be and how we feel they shaped us the past, thus freeing up energy in the now. If you need to address a nagging issue of unforgiveness within, try the following exercise.

Take a moment to close your eyes and visualize the past. Allow your mind the freedom to free associate ideas that are coming to it. You will find that the *unforgiven* memories come to the surface most readily. This is because they come under the scrutiny of the mind time and time again. Know that, through God's love, you have the ability to instantaneously heal these memories and to know complete forgiveness.

Truly, the forgiveness *we allow* in is an extension of the direct flow of God's love through us. Likewise, we can refuse to allow this loving flow. But, to experience the correction and release this flow in full forgiveness, we must surrender to God all the unresolved feelings and thoughts of the memory or memories. To allow surrender is to say of unforgiveness, in uplifted offering, "I don't know how to release this, but I know I want to be released from it. Please show me how to be..." In this growth space, God can gift you lifeforce...the ability to know the deeper truth of who you are. When you surrender to it, stronger energy comes into the present through the release of the past. Then right action, living as it was meant to be *for today,* flows through your life more smoothly. The life-energy blockage is gone!

Until we are standing in the truth of love, we will not know forgiveness. It hides in Divine memory, beyond emotional wrestling, waiting for us to uncover it. Yet emotionally trying times in our lives can lead to the uncovering of forgiveness—of purity. Some may ask, *"Why do all that searching?"* you ask. Perhaps the simplest answer to this question is just that, through our searching, there is something very precious to be found...

Each of us has a deep, internal barometer and *release mechanism* to our emotions. Wholesome wellbeing depends upon the proper rate and quantity of emotional release. For some, this release mechanism must be triggered at a deeper level than for others...through effortful activities such as therapy, counseling, reaching out to friends for support, reading, attendance of workshops, etc.

On a mental level, forgiveness means having the awareness that in the past you did not have all the tools of discernment you needed to function from the highest and best place within yourself. In your mind, you also had to deal with a multitude of voices that judged all the choices you made or didn't make. Are we not our own worst critics? Until we come to a greater knowing of truth, it can be quite challenging to discern between which voices are truth and which are generated by your fears, or your unforgiveness towards self and others.

In forgiveness we must reach a level of partnership or friendship with ourselves that acknowledges that we have shown up to let love in. This *is not* an external idea about making changes so that we can feel happier. To see the greater picture, we have to backtrack to the original misperception of thinking that the solution dwelt in our external lives, and shift it inward.

Awareness within is the open spaces of the heart found in forgiveness...layers of buds waiting patiently to open into a profusion of fragrant flowers. Try to see the internal as a wide open space of freedom within the space of acceptance and forgiveness. It is all right and it is all learning, so now the shifts we make do not have to be *ego clobbered* in our minds; rather, seek to accept them as part of the great learning process.

The mind's concept of life is a pulling action-much external motion using experiences to polarize one's existence into right, wrong, good, bad, etc. The ego mind or "little I" cannot fathom how it would be to enter into stillness, where pure love essence can connect in our hearts...to see something and to *not* judge it...to forgive everywhere...and to not waste another minute of life in thinking we need to know it all. Our minds are incredible storehouses of information from our lives, and as we forgive ourselves we free up the mind to more fully live in its creative capacities.

Complete forgiveness will always be the point of reference within ourselves for love. When we can forgive ourselves, we are in the action of loving and we don't have to fall prey to emotions stemming from a sense of lack or failure. Here, compassion will naturally begin to emanate from us in all our interactions. Here, we will also see the acute need for compassion and forgiveness in the world, and we'll begin helping others by forgiving them in their humanness from the open spaces of our heart(s).

I fight with my human condition, and I fight with that of others as I fear seeing it in them. Admittedly, I have spent much of my life running from who I am in fear, instead of seeing that I came here to grow and to reach towards the light. In this recognition I can begin to forgive and to feel more whole.

When I can see myself in a place of forgiveness, I will naturally be able to forgive others. These healing actions generate more love and happiness in my life and in the lives of those around me. My actions from the past have all been based on a greater need and desire to feel more love in my life…period.

I need to accept that I am human, and in my human form I do not recognize perfection and so at times I feel a sense of lack. With the essence of forgiveness I can look at my human limitation in a place of acceptance and offer love out of this place, knowing I am not any different in my humanness than all those around me, and knowing that love can heal the pain of that sense of separation from others that I sometimes, most humanly, can feel.

PART II

The Garden of Springtime: Planting the Seeds of Love Within

Sometimes...
Would you love God just sometimes?
When you love someone truly, are you just loving them sometimes?
The love of God is inside of you. Would you love yourself just sometimes?
If love has many, many faces of expression, why would you deny yourself so many of them?
See someone you love dearly in your mind's eye.
See how you can love them in all their ways, through their many expressions.
The love is constant. Even when you take time apart, the love is constant.
God's heartbeat is your heartbeat
Your body, His temple.
Would you love this sometimes? Oh, now I see it:
Self-judgment and criticism live only in the mind.

Chapter Five

Accepting and Loving Ourselves

The richest love within us begins on the shores of the deepest inner investigation, where no *"I'm not good enough"* self-talk can continue to hold ground in the "I Am" concept. We may have had many false starts at this new type of love, but we all have the potential to come to wholeness of self-love no matter how slow our journey towards it. Then, as we love ourselves, our outworn perception of the world also changes.

To recap, from a spiritual perspective, the central shift in self-love is the awareness of sensing God-energy, when we remember it, *everywhere*—even within ourselves as we realize that we are a part of the greater whole of existence.

Spirit is found on the pathway toward meeting ourselves. On this pathway, there is a mist just beyond our eyesight…a gentle magnet coaxing us to feel its pull. As we start to comprehend the deeper ocean of self, we will meet with satisfaction and self-regeneration time and time again. The guides and angels through the love-awakened doorway have called out to each one of us across all time. It has been only our forgetting that has dulled our awareness of them. But now the calling to again fully know Spirit's love is here.

If we could talk to God about self-love now, perhaps, He would say, "The fullest way to know Me is to feel my love within yourself. Feel it for all that you are, and feel it for all of life from there. When you have glimpsed this love within you, then grace will touch you and, each time, you will bring that love out into the world."

Globally speaking, our world is hungry for love and compassion as never before. Likewise, extending love through awareness of Spirit assists us in ways we cannot even fathom. As we begin to move more fully with God, we naturally extend service and assistance to others—benefiting both them and ourselves...

We have been taught that the way to help in this world is to give unselfishly of ourselves. We give of our time or give monetarily to causes and, while this is immeasurably helpful, there are even deeper, more impactful ways of assisting in the world situation. Let me explain...

Giving from the heart is the deepest form of giving. Here, you are connecting in God essence with other people. Yet to give from the heart, the starting point must be a sense of *love connection* to who you are deep within. When you feel love inside yourself, you express it more fully as you move to assist others and to work for the good of the planet—and you also become a conduit for that love. You now help by being a message of light to others in darkness who also need and seek love.

Love is an open playing field of learning. To integrate love into our lives at the greatest depth, we must first go to the foundation of our hearts. To love others sincerely, we must first begin to love ourselves within. For some, this thought may be troubling. Perhaps your life experience and past relationships have not taught you a great deal about how to practice love, and even the very concepts of self-worth and self-love may be foreign to you. Don't despair.

The beginning point to the emanation of love is simply to start right now. To believe that you can go the distance you are meant to go in this life, you first need to accept where you are right now. Do you have trouble accepting? Accepting is your first step, but keep going! Through imperfections, doubts, insecurities, and fears you can still reach inward and find love.

A Simple Truth

Your ability to love yourself does not depend on having a partner in your life; that is an added bonus! The people in your life that you care most deeply for can receive only the degree of love that you practice towards yourself.

We have to make a supreme effort to love ourselves *fully*. We may think we are loving, honoring, and caring for ourselves, but when we take a good look at our lives, how kind are we to ourselves? Do we exercise simplicity in our lives? Do we honor our bodies as much as we can? Are we truthful to ourselves about what truly works for us, and what doesn't? Do we take action on it?

Changes in oneself don't come overnight, even when we feel ready to make them. Steady progress, full of effort, will yield the desired results.

To birth greater self-love, there must be acceptance of who we are and of what the conditions of our lives are at this moment. Paradoxically, self-acceptance does not take away from our ability to love others; it increases it tenfold. And as we recognize within our own selves the deeper levels of who we are, we are free to see others from a more nonjudgmental perspective.

We tap into our own sense of strength.

At earlier stages in our lives, we have all had to strive to know love more deeply. Somewhere in our consciousness, there has been the deepest longing in all of us of wanting to be found in love, first by our parents, and then by those whom we began to love as we advanced in our journey toward independence, formulated a notion of who we were, and acted that out in hopes of making the formula complete. The problem is that we were not *mind readers*, so it was easy to have miscommunications when we felt afraid or didn't have the tools to ask for what we needed.

When you look back, there may be a strong memory of when you felt the intense desire for love that you felt was not being returned. You may have tried to be different, or tried to be more than, hoping you would be noticed. You were hoping you would be found; a rare and treasured pearl adrift within the sea of life. This may have started a tape running in your mind about your own definition of love, and how you felt you were inadequate to receive it. As an adult, you still run the tapes of long ago at times and you feel you come up short.

Now, beyond all those taped voices that told you who you were and why you were unworthy, can you dare to be all that you truly are today? Will you commit to *yourself* to help birth this essence inside of you—a person who, moment to moment, knows best what their most natural path for this life is?

In recognizing this person, you take up residence in your favorite soft, cotton shirt, and come to realize all the comforts that go along naturally with being at home with yourself! In all our present daily interactions, we will draw towards us the level of limitation we place on love within us. Thus, the more we can know of the richness of love, the more we will draw in healthy relationships.

As adults, what we think others may be thinking of us cannot provide a steady sense of safety in our lives. This is because the mind is always moving from thought to thought, fear to fear, insecurity to insecurity. Yet there is a also a constant supply of love in our hearts, and to have this love fully functioning for us in our relationships, we must first uncover a knowing of the essence of the love that we are—the truth of our intimate connection to God. In this internal place, we smile a *real* smile, confident of what shines within us, and can also help others by truly listening and by holding eye contact that conveys truth and love.

The more simple our lives are, the more truth will be revealed to us. Without the usual distractions and busyness going all the time, we will start to hear the messages coming from *ourselves*. We'll start to listen to what lights us up, and hear what makes us happy. We'll start to sense that the happiness is more instinctive…springing from a feeling in the heart much more than a thought in the head.

In the more quiet corners of our lives, we can find a knowing that there is an inherent "goodness" in each of us. It is a state in which we don't have to do anything or act in a special way. We have a place in us that knows we are good enough to be in this world just as we are. When we can love ourselves through even our sense of fault, we are gifting all who we are in contact with the opportunity to experience the same within themselves and carrying a message of universal love. Try the following quiet exercise.

Feel the love within you now as complete. You are that complete love. Let yourself believe this as slowly or as quickly as you are able. This is a deep truth...the God-essence of happiness. Honor yourself at all times. Take time-outs from the hectic pace in your life and create good, decisive boundaries with others. Listen to yourself and to what your needs are, honoring them as important. Then you will be loving others as never before!

Tell God that you will believe that Divinity resides in you, even if you can't see or sense it for now. Now you have made room to begin a new experience in your sense of self. The experience of loving ourselves is actually many subtle experiences that add up to a greater sense of growth happening. We must want to see ourselves without all the self-criticism we are used to hearing from our minds.

What we tell ourselves, we are used to taking out into the world to prove is right. It's as if we walk around with others reading from scripts that say, "You are really not good enough!" ...and we then swap scripts with others. This amplifies a sense of lack within. We all want some sense of direction in our lives. Who wouldn't? But it is we alone who don't let ourselves see that we can rewrite our scripts whenever we choose, that we have the power and authority to know within ourselves, and to share with others, who we are.

Rewriting the Scripts of the Past

The deeper self-love that we are birthing inside of ourselves will have a much stronger, deeper resonance than, *"I promise myself to start that exercise program tomorrow,"* or *"I really shouldn't be so hard on myself all the time."* What we desire is to lay a new foundation of personal trust so that we are approaching ourselves in a fuller expression of who we are underneath all our layers of fear and blindness. We lay the new foundation...by making more room to listen inwardly to ourselves. Laying the foundation is unique to each one of us because it is based on rewriting the scripts from the past that still sabotage us today. Though changes in self don't come overnight, steady, effortful progress will yield the desired results.

A Simple Truth

Your voice is important. It is vital.
Your ability to communicate truth to yourself remains within you. It springs from the innocence you knew before the adult persona grew to full force.

The beginning of rewriting the scripts of the past in our minds is to return to the innocence that exists within us all. By really listening to the still, small voice within us, in time we will come to know the truth of the love that we are. It may take some time before this action feels natural to us because it actually requires having a conversation with ourselves. Practice this activity with the exercise that follows.

Slow yourself down and become observant. Start to listen to yourself and what is taking place in your life...without judging.

You are finding the voice within you of wanting. Listen. Even if you feel like you are just starting to learn how to communicate, listen. Your voice of innocence has so much to tell you about the wanting. Wanting has needs down deep that have to be heard in order to find wholeness. Be patient. Truly listen…many times.

As you listen, remind yourself of the love that you are…beyond all the adult voices. This reinforces the strength of love within you. With time and practice, you will learn how to hear the wanting and to truly discern ways to comfortably satisfy your needs today. Remember that when you are fueled with love inwardly, you will naturally be more giving and present to others.

We may not hear clear answers right away, but this voice of want and need dwells inside of each one of us, and it can be critically accessed. Because love rests on a foundation, when it is recognized within it asks us to take responsibility for it in our lives in order to keep it alive.

The truth is that we have been experiencing love from a sense of lack. We are now shifting to know it from the inexhaustible resource of Spirit, who makes Himself known to our hearts as we open to new experiences. This is different from what we have known of the model of romantic love. It is learning to love from the inside outward. This love is steadfast and, as we learn to let it grow, is a gift to all humanity. It is slow to grow, but it is permanent—to the enhancement of our lives!

How do you love yourself more fully? By acknowledging the constant motion of life and by making peace with it, realizing you can move with it because it is you who create your own experiences.

Consider yourself closely when you are making your next decision. This is a leap in self-awareness and self-love. You have the first right of refusal in your own life and space. Saying no sometimes just means a time-out in life to sense what's best for you. Listen to what you need.

Now you will have made room to begin a new experience in your sense of self.

Why try to be anything other than who you are? Apply love to what you do, and you will learn a whole new way of being in this world. When this happens, it is a miracle of sorts. It is a rewriting of your life's script according to the new energies that you have allowed in.

*You are the beauty
shining through the darkest of night.
Your body only waits for you
to love it fully
in all its impermanence.
Ask it, "What can I give to you now
That I may know and better honor you?"
Just say that-no more.
And let your body respond,
"Just love me,
just love me."
Can you hear that?*

Chapter Six

Experiencing Soul Beauty

The jewel of knowing love within is soul beauty. It starts with a single point of light and, as I focus more and more, becomes multifaceted. Tentative in my discovery of myself as love, at first I wear the jewel for a time, taking it off and putting it on again. As it grows in brilliance in response to my heart's resonance, I discover that I have it with me all the time. It shines outward from within me. The deeper my love grows, I know and feel it as one with my heart—radiant and everlasting.

Just as we come to deepen our awareness of Spirit's connection to all, we can know true beauty. There is a depth of beauty to all of us that moves far beyond what we have learned. To begin to know ourselves from the love and light of God within us expands us in the beautiful awareness of many shimmering layers. These layers are the subtle bodies of energy that make up who we are, emanating from the soul at our center.

Beauty—the kind of beauty we mean here—is of course pleasing to the natural eye, but its real value emanates energetically outward from the heart's center. Beauty, we soon see, only becomes real in the process of our discovering it within ourselves. It surprises us over and over again—just as love does! This is true joy, and it is ours. The jewel we become is formed as we begin to sense how alive our soul shines through our bodies, fed by the awareness of heart-energy we can introduce over and over through self-love's doorway.

When beauty can be experienced in this way, it can change how we feel in the world. Because through God our soul's interior beauty is connected to beauty everywhere, we will sense that we are living life without having to try so hard. We soon become more fluid in our actions and more energized—just by knowing the beauty inside of us.

Culture encourages us to evaluate first and foremost a sense of who we are based on our physical appearance and on what we project outwardly. While this is motivational to our stance and outward approach in life, it cannot provide our sense of self with enough constancy to support the inward love emanating from the heart.

Beauty has its own perfect ordering. When we are not happy with our bodies or how we look it's because we are not treating ourselves with full respect and reverance. All we need to do is cultivate our Divine awareness within which will automatically re-order our bodies over time to exactly the state that would reflect it. Our innermost awareness of our own Divinity heals the body to the state where grace can flow in and out.

We have relied on the outer world to define what our beauty was, but the outer world is susceptible to people's mood swings, the latest fad, the weather, the media, and so on. Being swayed by outer influences makes us prone to drama in our lives because we are tapped into an unstable energy current that is supported by judgment and fear, not love.

It is hard for many to accept that simple beauty, at its peak of perfection, is part of who we are right now. Everything from how we smile inwardly, to how we communicate and feel, to how we care for ourselves, to all our passions, to the colors we are drawn to, to the places we love to go and the foods we love…is all an extension of the inherent loveliness that is within each one of us.

From the raw rock of cultural messages imbedded within us at a certain age, which define beauty materialistically or visually, we can chip away at the idea and find new jewels of thought on beauty that truly inspire. These messages let us know that incredible beauty lies within each one of us and is able to be enjoyed in many ways…at any age, or in whatever physical form we are…as long as we feel good and balanced within ourselves.

A Simple Truth

*When we know we are connected to a shine
inside of us that is permanent,
it invites others to enjoy the experience of itself,
and rarely needs repolishing!*

True beauty is integrity and authenticity. Integrity is an expression of soul beauty. It is an action I keep within myself, in *my* heart, which allows me to show up for life as I Am…in *my* true colors—not looking to change myself, nor to change others. Here I have invited myself, with the deep compassion of my heart, to experience all of life. It is the grace with which royalty takes a bow, and the sincere heart with which a hand is extended to offer to another its assistance. Although true beauty knows humility, it will not apologize for appearing in imperfection, for it knows only the sense of its own imperfection can cloak it in true humility.

Soul beauty would go and dance in fear, knowing that fear

can be transcended …that the body will age…and that it does not go with us from this life into the next, but that the soul moves powerfully through all. To know the soul, then, brings the essence of eternal beauty forth.

Soul beauty speaks for itself when we remember who we are-even down to the cellular level. This awareness of beauty is not an attempt to produce an imaginary experience. It is, rather, an internal part of us breathing the knowledge of beauty into our souls, into the physical body through heart-energy. Those who've comprehended this beauty have recognized somewhere within themselves the powerful seeds of who they are at a soul level. And they have come to understand that the physical body and the expression of soul essence are not separate.

Sensing Soul Beauty…

- There is depth and clarity; light in our eyes.
- We stand taller and hold our head higher.
- We focus better on other people and tasks.
- Our expressions and gestures are more spontaneous.
- The tone of our voice may shift, or we may speak more slowly.

Feeling Soul Beauty Within…

- We are serene.

- We are confident.
- There is less stress weighing our every thought.
- We know love as direct experience.

Cultivating Soul Beauty is…

- Seeking larger awareness.
- Reminding ourselves that we are expressions of love.
- Making choices that emanate self-value.

Love every part of yourself, no matter what your age or size! When you can do this, the love you feel will be more real to you than anything you have experienced on earth thus far because it is the blending of the soul and the physical body—the infinite and the finite, through the expression of unconditional love.

Love your body! Don't wait another second to acknowledge it. Let it take you through the amazing gift of this earth journey. Be fully alive in body on a soul level, aware of the light within you, and it will gift you unconditional, compassionate love—born to self, but expanding unbounded in all with whom you come into contact!

Through lifetimes the angels wait patiently that we might tune into and hear their assistance as we grow to meet ourselves in the gift of beauty. We meet ourselves as we accept the truth that we are alive in our laughter as well as our tears, in our triumphs, as well as our difficulties. We are complete in our awareness of beauty.

In the responsible acceptance of ourselves in adulthood,

where we are no longer acting out every drama that comes into our lives, we begin to feel the fuller essence of being a man or being a woman. Spirit reveals more and more depth to us, because we have found ourselves more fully in simplicity.

If you are granted sight of what beauty, below its surface presentation, truly is, you start to see beauty everywhere…because beauty is true *God vibration* through matter. It is a blessing to be gifted this sight or awareness. Once you are gifted this sight, you will return again and again to feel this sight more deeply within you. It will reach into your essence to want to awaken you more deeply to your own beauty…because it is a magnetic resonance that wants to know itself more deeply.

This vision of beauty refines every picture, every person, and every moment in time that it touches. It brings into super high resolution the things we had seen before but now see with awakened eyes-so that there is a new depth to people, to nature, and to our surroundings. It is an essential sight, and in this sight a miracle takes place. The covering that holds the beauty breaks apart to give way to the greater sight. Where the greater sight is seen, things begin to shift and new possibilities surface.

The new possibilities want only to birth truth and to move past the confinements of our linear mind's thoughts. They allow us to move in the world and to tackle projects in increments, to see relationships in a different light, and to move through obstacles with each other with greater ease and less effort than we've ever known.

A Simple Truth

*We are all good enough and beautiful enough.
We are all just right, right now!
We are worthy of being loved and accepted,
even at our very most vulnerable.*

If someone shies away from us because we are showing our true colors, it's probably because they have a deep fear of seeing their own. Tell yourself, *"Even feeling vulnerable, still I Am that beauty, that work of art, that written prose, because it emerges from the depths of me. I go about and discover it continually as I live it. The person I Am does not have to be seen as separate from my expression in the world. I Am my expression, so I want to make it count!"*

Renewal

Renewal in beauty and serenity is not dependent on what our bodies look like, or on how old we are, or on how we compare ourselves to the world that we see with our tinted glasses. Renewal in beauty is dependent on what our cells, our body and soul cells, when integrated, hunger for: extra time, more peace, presence to ourselves, soothing moments, calming spaces, and breathing the love within us.

I so need both to be renewed and to be renewing…each and every moment. Life is not an experience that I must get right to feel that I am fully here…at last. The deepest beauty message I can give to myself is the message of renewal, over and over…as many times as I want and need it. Here is a simple affirmation to deepen your awareness. Reflect:

"My renewal awaits me. I come up for air. I reconsider. I bathe in the cleansing waters of Spirit. I release my cares to the wind. I let go with force the fire in my mind in order to transmute negativity and energize myself. Renewal is my gift, always."

Think of all the seeds lying inside of us… waiting gently for us to release them. Every time we acknowledge to ourselves the strength of who we are in love and the depth of our soul beauty, these seeds are inspired to stir, to sprout, and to grow freely.

A lesson in beauty...

Slow down. Appreciate the way you move through your actions.
Slow down. Let yourself acknowledge your gifted body.
Understand that outward messaging about your body is an illusion.
You are the inner dictator of how you feel about yourself.
All of your self-doubt is about fear.
Afraid to be seen as you are,
Others fear to be seen, too—just like you, no matter their appearance.
When you feel self-conscious, look towards another and let yourself hear
their fear about themselves...
It is no different than your own fear.
Now you can say inwardly, "My fear is a false barrier I have built around my expression.
My expression is my beauty. My expression is free as a bird.
It is the sunlit path, the laughing path of my soul.
God has gifted me awareness, here and now, of joyful expression through
imagined boundaries that I thought held me fast.
I will accept that everyone has the same fears that I do.
I will accept that if I push past my fears, I hand them the key to the door of their inner freedom to do the same.
The expression of love will surface naturally and perfectly for each situation.
We just need to look past the fear...with eyes of love...and we will be
aware of our true beauty.

PART III

Tending and Growing the Garden in All Seasons

*The True desireless
is a face of God
moving forward,
ever moving...
hands open, empty,
heart full of the Divine...
walking in the utmost of grace,
natural...
not escaping from body,
fully entered into it all,
and experiencing its joy!
Know that beyond the mantle of the body,
there is the expression of Spirit...
of Soul into matter*

*The mind must align to it,
for it can do nothing else.
Now the body is not held prisoner
to the mind.*

*I have promised my soul
to give it full welcoming
in this body temple of mine—
humility below the depth of depths,
vastly present and deep
for the gift that allows my sight
and knowing
of my soul incarnate.*

*My soul would have me
Sing through all time!
So I must keep to
the disciplines of caring for
my body temple,
which houses my soul here on earth,
then let my soul express
from this place,
this space...
Moment by moment to feel the love
Ever present within...
the joy
within.*

Chapter Seven

Walking in Balance

From a place of internal balance we are more able to spend time in devotion and awareness, which brings us more in touch with Spirit communication on many levels. To show up fully present in this life, our mind, body, and soul need to walk in balance. Walking in balance promotes the strongest expression of ourselves here on earth. If we intend to express the full love that we are, walking in balance, an extension of moving towards that fulfillment, must be our priority.

As we come to understand that we are connected to an infinite Source of energy that is God, we may go through periods where we want to go up, up, and away in that energy, that thrilling awareness or sense of connection. Unfortunately, there is no way to do that and also to fully tend to our bodies and duties in the physical world at the same time.

Yes, we can be ever-present in our connection to God, but we must maintain balance through time intervals set aside for seeking guidance or inner communion—our spiritual practices of choice—and time periods for actively living out our purpose in this life.

One level of rhythm that is key to finding balance are the periods we create for activity and inactivity. There are times we are called to seek God more fully…and then times when we feel His presence sweep through our lives simply because we were open to receive Him. This balance enhances our awareness of ourselves in wholeness—in male/female aspects.

We seek spiritual practice because it is a tangible reminder that God is an integral part of our lives. The energetic strength brought in by regular time in communion with Spirit will open the doorway to many horizons we have yet to discover.

When we are actively deepening our awareness and seeking, our spiritual practice may include: attending organized services, prayer, meditation, reading sacred text or spiritual writings, chanting, contemplation, yoga, spending time outdoors. It is the regularity of the discipline, no matter how simple or intense, that creates more balance in our life.

A Simple Truth

With regularity in seeking,
you will sense subtleties surfacing.
You will notice many elements and visuals in your life
that you hadn't even seen or sensed before.
It will feel new and promising.
It may feel quiet and serene, too.

Your expression of yourself in this world is a precious thing. What you bring forward in this life from within you deserves airtime, deserves your sense of inner renewal. It deserves your commitment to yourself through your spiritual practices.

Of course there will be times when situations arise or times of chaos when it seems impossible to keep to a regular self-care and spiritual routine. In difficult times, there might be a tendency to cast all the practices or routines aside and to throw up our arms. The challenge is to remain as focused as possible when faced with difficulty. Here, trust will be needed more than ever.

To take our newfound awareness out into the world, we also need the balance of a healthy diet, rest, and a sense of groundedness in our physical bodies. We can find this grounded and centered feeling through exercise, work outdoors, or preferred physical pursuits. We also want to stay plugged into a sense of our life's purpose, if possible, in a job or career that fuels our creativity and passion.

Some form of regular body or energetic healing work such as reiki or massage, for example, is important for us to stay cleansed and to clear our awareness of the energy within and around us. It may initially feel trivial to us to take time out in our schedule for this, especially if we feel pretty good. It's helpful to remember that these actions are *preventive* of disease or imbalance in the body. We don't want to wait until there is physical discomfort to seek the needed balance.

If we have let our busyness get the better of us, it's not too late to reclaim balance. Any deficit we feel in our lives is a sign or a cue that we need to readjust something and get back into balance. For example, if we are not feeling well we must first and foremost shift our awareness to the healing of our physical body. When our emotions are running strong, we will want to find a vent for them by reaching out to others. When we feel depleted spiritually, we must go more deeply into our personal practices.

Below surface awareness, we all walk around as constantly interacting energies. When we are consciously aware, our soul body blends with energy-raising to the degree that we are accepting of and knowing it. Our soul body emanates the degree of light within our physical body and shifts higher in energy as we grow in consciousness.

The action of our energies blending with our interactions with others is subtle, but strong. Because energy is always moving, we want to stay in harmony with it. This means keeping our energy field clear and bright with light while staying centered, grounded, and focused in the physical body.

Emotionally or mentally repetitious thoughts are honored and shifted most by being heard. They run through us and have no pattern of stability to them. Our inner strength to have balance depends on the light that is constant beneath those thoughts. Try the following exercise to increase your awareness of the power of your own thoughts:

Listen to what the mind has to say or wants to express without being pulled far off balance. Simply find the space to listen. As you listen to what your thoughts are saying, let yourself believe that you are helping these thoughts or feelings to find their way through. Believe that they will leave your mental space when they are ready, no matter how many times the same thought or emotion seems to circulate.

The same thing is true when nagging thoughts move towards behavior or habits that aren't for the best in our lives. We want to partner with what we are experiencing as much as possible. We want to be our own best friend, which can seem like a big internal step, since we are much more used to reaching outside of ourselves. When we know what it is that we are choosing and what fuels it, we can hear it out and walk through it to a new level.

Balance in our Environment

Keeping the external environment of our homes and our cars fairly clean and organized will help us to stay more focused and more balanced in our minds.

A Simple Truth

Your energy needs to be able to expand around the space you live in to gain a sense that you are fully at home there. Being at home in your home is one step closer to being more at home in your own skin.

If you are not used to feeling comfortable at home and you get a sense of this new energy now, gather it up into full consciousness. It is moving energy, helping you to expand yourself.

For the givers in this world who are regularly putting energy out to assist others, you will need your home to act as a sponge, soaking in your tiredness and worries and sending back love to you. It will also act as your shock absorber—to regulate relaxation apart from the dualities of the world.

There is no reason that your home cannot give you a sense of calm, of safety, of love, and of serenity. You need only to work with the energies of your home to get it the way you want it. Steer clear of clutter by throwing things out or giving away things that are no longer needed. Calming, warm colors, house plants, flowers, aromatherapy, different lighting, fabric textures, will all help you to create this haven that speaks to you and represents the energies with which you resonate. Of course your home *will* shift with changing energies, but over time it becomes a strong environmental tool to support the centeredness that you wish to structure into your life.

Living in balance requires us to be fully aware of our body's functioning as a total collaboration of its own state of mind and of the body/spirit connection; being fed by our *thought-forms*, as well as our body's physical state being nurtured tangibly. This includes seeking out appropriate rest, a balanced diet that supports health, and appropriate exercise to energize the body so that it can hold a fuller expression of love, light, and vibration. The more *vibrant* we are able to feel, the better able our cells are to absorb energy.

For Spirit to be interwoven and fully grounded within our being, our mind/body connection must be at its fullest capacity of balance. For example, we keep our thoughts as positive as we can. We receive healing work or energy work that keeps our energy clear. We can help clear out the cobwebs of old tapes running in our minds with meditation, listening to music, or chanting work. Affirmation work will help, also.

Remember first and foremost to give yourself permission internally to seek to feel more balanced. You are creating the positive for your life on many levels. You do not want to be harsh on yourself about seeking balance. All of our lives are busy enough!! What you are aiming to do is seek the balance in small amounts, but regularly, and *any* effort you make will make a difference in your life.

Sometimes it helps to feel motivated when you can picture clearly how the action you take helps you immediately; i.e., I am choosing to exercise because I know it will help me feel more in touch with my body....or I'm going to sing or chant now because I know it will help me get out of the worries in my mind.

A Simple Truth

Fully living in this body/this life the soul must be somewhat contracted to fit within the physical dimension. It will need to reach harmony within the physical to fully thrive here. If you can learn to more fully be your whole self here in this lifetime —without running as the responsibilities become greater— you will have amazing stories of love to share!

Basic Balance-Keeping Activities

The following are simple actions that can be taken to return to balance when necessary.

- Yoga or exercise in some regular routine
- Meditation
- Eating green food and fresh fruit (along with the rest of our diet)
- Getting out in the fresh air and breathing deeply
- Being gentle with yourself and with others
- Socializing and making room for laughter
- Drinking lots of water
- A solid, consistent sleep routine

Grounding Actions for when you feel high in God-energy:

- Connecting with others meaningfully…from the heart
- Doing projects that require focus
- Doing creative activities with friends, children, and/or pets
- Getting exercise outdoors
- Doing gardening
- Sitting under, leaning against, or hugging a tree
- Walking barefoot outside
- Swimming in a lake or the ocean
- Eating heavier food (more protein, carbohydrate)
- Singing out the energy. Love your voice!
- Playing a musical instrument

Suggested Activities for Stressed-Out Times:

- Meditate.
- Get your hands on any aromatherapy: Hand or body lotion, room mist, essential oil placed on pulse points, candles, incense…it doesn't have to get elaborate, just inhale and relax!
  Some examples of relaxing fragrances are: lavender, chamomile, sandalwood, jasmine, honeysuckle, vanilla.
- Take a quiet walk or listen to instrumental music; tune out larger noises.
- Avoid crowded places.
- Take a nap, even if it's only for ten minutes in a chair.
- Talk to God, or chant.

· Sing from the heart in your car, outdoors, or anywhere—but really do it from down deep! This is very healing and releasing.
· Eat light and airy foods; avoid dense, refined junk foods.

When You Are Feeling Your Lowest:

· Let yourself cry, if you can.
· Get quiet and release your worries, cares, and concerns to God in prayer. Feel yourself surrender your deepest fears, pain, or concern.
· Assess your level of tiredness and get sleep right away if that's what your body tells you it needs.
· Talk to a friend that you trust.
· Get into the sunlight for ten minutes or more.
· Listen to a radio station you would ordinarily never tune in.
· Get a massage…or rub your own feet!
· Have a fresh fruit drink.
· Talk to the moon or gaze at the stars.

To Connect More Fully to Your Soul's Beauty:

· Observe and connect with children.
· Use discernment to create simplicity in your life.
· Move your body…*dance!*
· Spend time in silence.
· Spend time in nature.
· Listen to or create beautiful melodies.
· Speak your truth as often as you can….and feel your words!

- Uncover your life's purpose or your passions—then start to live them.
- Share your love in intimacy with another.
- Explore sacred sexuality.
- Share hugs and laughter.
- Feel your connectedness with the earth, go for walks.
- Travel to sacred places.

*How much growing
will you do in this lifetime?
What does it mean to
your body, your mind, your soul?
What does it mean to
the broad expanse of
their expression combined?
What does aliveness mean to you?*

Chapter Eight

Growth Spurts

Spirit will hand you learning opportunities with others of all kinds so that you can grow in love. But keep in mind that growth is both an action *and* a process. In the action of growth we are choosing to *again and again* allow shifts and change in our lives. This involves the effort of showing up within ourselves. In growth spurts we know that, although we are in a sometimes-challenging process, more self-love is emerging, which generates positive energy.

God gifts us new scenes in our lives for the purpose of our growth. The direction of our movement forward may not even be shown to us. In some instances we may be shown flashes into the future. Growth experiences may present themselves as health issues, relationship issues, issues around career shifts, and so on. Again, the growth work will always lead us to a deeper sense of who we are, and as we discover this true person we will naturally be drawn to live our lives in the place of balance.

A Simple Truth

From a place of balance, we are more able to spend time in devotion and awareness, which brings us more in touch with spirit communication and blessings on many levels.

Experiences will continually be presented to us. It is completely up to us how we choose to order them through our lives. And if we don't block it with our minds, growth will naturally flow. New ways of approaching old patterns will become apparent to us. We don't have to feel like any one pattern of "stuckness" has a hold over us. We begin to see the pattern for what it is—a holding pattern for ego safety's sake.

No matter the circumstances we find ourselves in, we need to know that we are the key-holders to making changes. The decision to surrender in our minds and allow ourselves to grow is always and only our own. At times, we may consider the cost and decide, for the time being, not to grow consciously...yet opportunities to do so will continue to be presented to us.

Some of the deepest growth we will ever experience springs from emotional difficulties. What seems unfair in this life is really not unfair—it is just that area of growing that wants to sprout in us. Our resistance to it is what is feeling unfair. Strangely, we attack ourselves with situations that our whole self drew into our lives for our soul's growth.

Many people walk around feeling, using, and expressing only a fraction of who they are in all their fullness. The persona that they feel is their whole self is starved for more love light energy. The irony is that their lack of awareness of this pulls them into relationships that force them to be who they are not and into unnatural situations, looking for the fullness of love. Love fullness cannot be found in the reservoir of someone else's life. We will not find it there when we have not first recognized it within our own selves!

Most people want more than anything else to feel loved and loving. The recognition that love is within ourselves feels scary or makes us angry because it feels like pulling it out will require an intense uphill climb. In our human condition, we share the same similarities. We all want to feel love more than anything else, but our minds continue to reinforce that it is found outside of us.

This type of wanting and desire simply cannot be satiated. We run around in an exhausting maze as we continue to chase after it.

Ego creates safety structures in the mind of what life "should" look like concerning job, family, appearance, anything…really. If we can step outside of one of those structures and see it for what it is; the pushing and critical nature of the structures we have built, we can move it to one side in our mind's eye as an observer. Here we are creating a very deep layer for internal change; one of the very most critical components to growth.

Thoughts move wildly from the past to the future. We are so concerned about the things spinning in our minds that we cannot seem to get a break and let ourselves be in the present, where we can free ourselves up to observe.

The challenge that we all face is the challenge of living in the spaces of duality. Duality rises out of the magnet of polarization in our lives. We can think of it as when our minds feel pulled into an "either/or" condition or into black and white thinking. A strong example is our feeling that we fail, or that we need to have something be "perfect" so that it feels acceptable.

The natural flow beyond duality is the flow of love, and when we are conscious about knowing Spirit more deeply in our lives, new experiences, people, places and things will undoubtedly surface more quickly in our lives in order for us to actively walk through our growth. When growth comes unexpectedly, it can feel very challenging.

When a challenge is presented to you, ask why. What are others telling you it is? Does society or media give a consistent message of this? Go within and ask yourself how it is a challenge, and then allow yourself to act on it in ways you feel you can. Remember that little steps amount to covering a lot of ground. Be gentle. Truth is wanting to reveal itself through the difficulties. Remember to trust, and it will give you the confidence to get through new experiences.

It comes to a point, where you will be able to say, "Why am I being so hard on myself if the learning is always happening? Now say to yourself, "I am here to grow in love awareness, and I am always moving towards it. I will stay out of self criticism."

When you can see the structures based on judgments of self and others that your mind created, you are beginning to let go of the structure that held you so tightly wrapped in limited expression and past and future tense. It is a process of taking walls down. These walls have served a protective purpose to your "Little I," of feeling safe in conformity. It may have felt like a form of sustenance. Still, you are here now with the structure to the side, because Spirit has called you forward.

The God-current has presented to you, in essence, to replace the ego structure walls with walls of effervescent light that fuel you with love-energy. By choosing to walk away from your ego wall structures; the "should" voices of judgment, you have accepted an invitation from Spirit to let love-energy enter in direct conscious connection to all that you are. Where learning is actively happening there are no *shoulds*.

Remember that flows of growth move in simplicity, so the simpler we keep our lives, the more we are "becoming." The mind moves in to complicate the simplicity by bringing in old patterns of hurt or high drama because it is afraid. Television soap operas are an extreme illustration of the dramas and pushing and pulling that can happen in fear! Ego, or "little I," is most afraid of change or anything that is brand new.

When the mind complicates, situations can take on a life of their own. We feel the pressure mounting in indecision, mood shifts, stress, insomnia, and eventually we may turn to reach for some form of escape through unhealthy habits, addictive patterns, or simply *tuning out*.

Growing pains come because we don't know what change will feel like; how it will present itself in us and in our lives. You only see a blank slate as scary, because you have not been here before. Ego mind will want to scurry around to add all kinds of extra color to the paint palette.

The colors, as emotion, are experienced so rapidly that they blend together and create confusion. The only way the mind can process the overload is to invent the system of good and bad, right and wrong. Under this system that the mind invented, all one's spirit can do is break against it.

The mind would rather give in to temptation time and time again. In the wars that are fought in the mind, there can be no peace. It's when we're not looking, when we've somehow let go, that life is happening at its fullest. There is no real way to know whether or not you are on the right track because the *right track* is exactly where you are right now, no matter your opinion of it. It is exactly where you are and exactly where you're meant to be.

The degree to which we show up fully in our lives determines the quality level that we live at, and the value we place on it. Any effort at all is an effort. Any action of seeking truth or taking moments to meditate or reflect, to reach out to others, makes a lasting connection. Resistance, like a set of overworn brakes of a car, may slow the growth process down a whole lot, but it will not completely stop the process.

We will feel positive in our growing processes when we can handle the growth and choices in two ways. First, we can make the effort to stay in touch with the heart-center energy each day. We do this by acknowledging our connection to God and that we have shown up to fully experience love. Secondly, we can move through our actions in authenticity to that love, by being self-accepting and non-judgemental towards others.

If we look for approval from the outside; what others think, we cannot feel a sense of wholeness within. Every single person around us will each see us differently, no matter what we are doing or wanting to represent.

Increments of growth and self-development occur in cycles as they are meant to and they unfold in such a way that we might not sense the growth happening. We can be grateful that there is this delicate golden weaving of assistance and positive energy all through our lives as we reach to better ourselves in spiritual awareness. In growth, we cannot be attached to immediate results. We use discernment so we stay in balance, where growth can occur.

Spiritual growth is a series of little births happening within us. Each birth elevates us away from ego when it occurs. Now what do we do in elevation with "little I," or ego staring at us from the distance and wanting attention? First, recognize that growth has occurred. Let yourself hear yourself speak inwardly from this new space. Conscious growth will show you that you are being moved more towards non-judgment of yourself and others into a loving constant of "all is well." Sometimes the "all is well" is fleeting, and sometimes it stays with us for the length of time we need to know that this state of Being really does exist. It's all the little birthings of "ahas" that make up the celebration of life.

When we reach this point in our lives where we have deep inner growth, we will have planted a sustenance that we cannot lose again. We may have setbacks or difficult times, but once the level of growth has been reached, we cannot lose it in the sea of our lives' future activity. This is because true growth occurs in the present moment, which is our anchor to the conscious experience of all that we are.

God is our silent witness, and so knows as we grow to know Him that we will bring Him to life within ourselves. When our concept of seeing stills from thought of past and future, we will see the humble majesty for that moment of time; the sense of God within.

Spirit is saying, "I want to share freedom with you. I want you to know how it is to just be, and to be non-attached to the smaller thoughts that hold you back from accepting me." We cannot fail to live fully if our heads are turned towards the future with our eyes open and our hearts willing to experience. We cannot fail. Here we are in the awareness of God as love and that is what is needed to fuel growth.

Your life can be anything you dream it to be. It is the focus of the dream that is the challenge, for when you set about to create the dream into being, then you are fully living. To dream and act, to explore life's motion, is to be alive. Honor within yourself that life is constantly shifting. To honor shifts of energy within you, no matter how they flow, will always create growth; the dawning of a new day for you. Simply trust Spirit to renew your sense of life time and time again. The circle of safety around you is so broad, it gives you plenty of room to explore all of life's possibilities…all of the directions that are open to you.

When I say, "I feel so stuck within myself."
Spirit would say, "Give me your hands and say, 'These hands I have created for growth. These hands can help me to move forward. They lead to my heart. I will remember who I Am when I reach out for help. Here Source can feed me from the bounty of love.'"
I reply to Spirit, "My walls will need to come down?"
"Yes, they will."
"These are walls I hold in place with everyone?"
"With everyone, yes, including yourself. It has blinded you from yourself."
"How do we do this?" I say.
"Removing one light, obstructing brick at a time."

Chapter Nine

Blocks of Resistance

Sometimes no matter how much we are striving towards spiritual growth in our lives, we will have periods of time when we can't sense Spirit much at all. Maybe we're questioning and doubting ourselves, resenting our positioning in life, or comparing ourselves to other people. Through our questioning and doubting, at times *ego mind* moves a big boulder of a question mark right in front of our faces.

"What is this? I want definition now," it says, *"And I want all the answers before you can leave this mental space."* Demanding immediate clarity, we cease to flow with the mysterious unfolding of Spirit.

Here we start to feel the distant tugging of our old ways—all the *"What ifs"* that have their basis in fear. We may feel like confusion is setting in, or experience sporadic mood swings that we can't make sense of. At such times, the mind will spin and spin!

Blocking is the point between, *"I cannot hear guidance at all. I feel so lost,"* and *"I am hearing the instruction, but I am not following it."* To flow with growth, we will need to go back to trust…walking forward in faith, even if it is blindly, moment by moment each day.

A Simple Truth

If you can commit yourself more fully to the life that you are seeking to let Spirit move in, you will eventually free movement away from the spinning of the mind.

We can make peace with our questions and doubts and work with ourselves besides—then we can feel the inward success of being able to move with ourselves in partnership with life.

Sometimes blocks manifest from external situations in our lives, whether we can control those circumstances or not. Some examples of this are:

· Needing to take medication for a physical ailment or condition that shifts us in clarity and focus, or depletes our energy level.

· Getting into a cycle of watching a lot of television, being on the computer a lot, or eating poorly.

· Experiencing an unexpected event in our lives that shakes our foundation.

When blocking and resistance feel very strong, we first want to check into our bodies. We cannot get to the place of heart opening if pain that is moveable is being held in the body. We will want to begin with self-care and self-awareness at the body level. This means balancing out our diet or putting harmful habits to rest in the now. It means getting rest in the now or easing a tension headache or sore shoulders or back.

When we are comfortable that the body is in reasonable balance, then we step into checking in with ourselves on the mental and emotional levels. Counseling may be helpful here, or talking productively to those we trust—whatever helps us to vent so that we can return to the starting-point of self-acceptance.

Remember, fear can only have a grip on us if we let it; otherwise it has to take its place in the background, where we have become its master, not allowing it to overrule our lives or the choices we make. Spiritual growth is a deep inward manifestation of God-awareness felt within. It surfaces in each one of us in its own perfect timing-as many times as we personally require it to do so in order to see and embrace new truth! It asks us to honor it, but it is also always there for us. Even when we resist it, it never leaves but gently waits for us to be ready for it in our awareness.

For us, definition has felt so important because when we define, we feel an experience is "ours," so we think we can't lose it. We feel we can *tag* its movement. It is a grand dilemma. We want so much to feel the love, but in growing we first have to do some digging, some rearranging within ourselves to find a love within us that moves past our definitions.

The good news is that when we stop in our lives because we feel an area, a relationship, a job, a course of study, etc. is at a standstill, in fact we are not stopping at all. We may have felt a need to believe there was a pause to catch our breath, but all the while, under every circumstance, new learning was unfolding. Indeed, we can believe that growth is happening for us right now, and that it will truly lead to stronger love connections with God, with ourselves, and with others.

We don't have to set a stringent standard or timetable for ourselves, which amounts to self-judgment. In one way or another, we are all *always* striving for a more meaningful life. This striving surpasses all the imagined standards we may feel the need to set.

Maximum Blocking

There may be times when the blocking or resistance in our minds leaves us feeling confused and as though we have no direction or solution to the pain we feel. When fear seemingly takes over in the mind, we might feel totally abandoned or threatened by the world around us. It may feel like we see our situation everywhere and in everyone. We can't get away from it. Our fearful situation takes on a *larger than life* quality. At this point, we may feel like we are standing in the middle of a dark forest at dusk with no way out.

In these moments, back up internally. Tell yourself that assistance is a belief away. Thoughts and fears build upon each other, and this is how things can begin to feel looming and overwhelming. Spirit can and will, however, offer you a different insight if you allow the shift in. It may help you to follow the pathway of this exercise:

Suspend judgment of where you are at first. Just tell yourself that this is not good or bad, right or wrong, or anyone's fault, at this moment. Move your thoughts down to your heart and let them breathe with the love light there. Accept that healing is always occurring from the spiritual realm if you allow it in. Now visualize that you are in a plane or a hot air balloon, high above the earth, but that God has given you insight into people's lives far below.

You observe many different scenes of things going on: Large families together, lovers, people quarrelling, people alone and together working in offices, elderly people alone or in groups together, children playing on playgrounds, families living in crowded cities without much income to support them, friends out celebrating a birthday, people working shifts in the middle of the night, traffic on the highway…

You are given this broader vision at this moment to remind you that it is just your own internal eyesight in your situation that makes it feel so large. There are many thousands of people in the world who share your difficulties on many different wavelengths. You are never, never alone in your suffering—no matter what you are going through. Guides and angels are just on the other side of your sight, there to take your troubles, and the troubles of so many others. Up in the air, with the view of everything below you, release your cares to the wind, knowing that even if your healing process is slow, God has created a new day for you to have clearer sight and to feel more love, no matter what it takes to get there.

Remind yourself about the energy that is constantly in motion around you, and that your life is shifting each and every minute, and that—having faith and trust—you can allow yourself to feel the sustenance that is yours for the taking…

A Simple Truth

*Each step you take towards this healing for yourself
is shaping a new reality or perhaps birthing a destiny in
your life. It is often not the earthshaking life event,
but the sequence of growth around the events that shapes
our internal fiber. Where we are internally
is what our life will bring forth to us.*

Understand that sight of ourselves has levels, and these levels are brought into view consciously as we let go into them…into the vision of how things exist in their pure state of being. When we surrender the unknown to God, our sight will deepen. The purity of new thought appears bright with light and it appears when we move past the "little I" within ourselves that holds on to definition and form.

When we block new insight that leads to growth, we are faced with the need to forgive ourselves or perhaps surrender to *"negative"* life circumstances. But we can mistakenly believe that in this surrender we would be lost. *In surrender we are found,* and are fully encircled by a thousand arms flung open and spread wide around us in complete joy. But to experience this loving embrace, we have to completely let go of expectation or definition.

Remember that you have chosen to write a new script for your life! You have never done this before, and so you cannot see what it will look like. When difficult days come up, there is a tendency for us to retreat to the safety of our minds—making all kinds of assumptions about the people or situations that we imagine are causing us pain. Yet we have no control over their lives, and in truth we have no idea what is happening with them, or what they may be experiencing emotionally, when we are not with them. It's a waste of energy and a vain fantasy to think that we fully know or understand another person's life!

Of course, we often imagine the "worst case scenario," or that which would cause us the most emotional strife. Painful past experiences, the memory of which is held fast in our minds, can cause us to operate from a place of fear. How can we assist ourselves in this area?

Remind yourself as often as you can, *"I am truly not aware of another person's full reality."* Let it all go now, any worries, just in this moment. Know that you cannot take responsibility for another adult's actions or life. God is working with them, just as with you, at whatever level is appropriate in the now. You can take responsibility for the choices *you* decide to make. Are you going to make decisions that keep you feeling stuck or in pain, or can you have faith that there is a better, more empowered life, one based on the freeing choices you will make, just waiting for you ahead?

In times of challenge, we also need to bring ourselves back to basics. When we were young children, our days and nights were filled with eating, sleeping, playtime indoors and out, or engrossed in various activities. As a child, it felt safe to have a good structure or a schedule that felt familiar. When we are in emotional challenges, it is really the child within us that is feeling vulnerable and afraid. At these times, structure may be a valuable container for fear and automatic negative responses.

Think of how simple it would be to take a fresh look at our time schedule and tighten it up, maybe to even map out our day structurally so that most of the decision-making is taken care of, and so are we! No matter how much is going on, make time within your schedule for that child within, and for meeting his or her comfort needs—whether it's having a bowl of soup, reading a few pages of a good book, walking in the park or, just for the fun of it, taking a new car for a test drive! Even in the busy workweek, we can find time for some of these activities…if we choose to make the time.

When we give to ourselves and feed the emotionally vulnerable areas within ourselves, we will feel a sense of safety emanating from within our own hearts. The tests and challenges that are a part of life on earth are very real, and no one alive is immune to them.

Sometimes talking with others for support is not enough because we may sense that they don't fully understand the depths of our challenges. We all need other people in our lives that we care about and that care about us, and hugs and conversations are wonderful *soul fuel.* We can also know in truth that there are so many ways for us to empower ourselves to make life more satisfying and less afflicted with the pain, sadness, or confusion we feel at times.

A Simple Truth

Realize on a new level that you are walking yourself through challenges, one at a time, and making it through them! Each and every one of us makes it through a challenge one step at a time, but it is certain that if we move with the assistance of love, we will see the results of growth, even through the darkest of times.

Prayer in Action: The Full Release of Prayer

When we pray we are seeking deep assistance or guidance from God. Trustfully, we project our words or thoughts outward in hopes of their being received. If we can think of prayer as an offering forth of energy, we can more fully unite with the God-awareness that will carry the intent of our prayer forward.

To set prayer in motion, get into your most comfortable praying position, whether it be sitting, kneeling, or lying down. As you think of your prayer, find the area of your body to which you feel it's connected. This may be your heart or your stomach, or it may be anywhere in your body. Now let your self-sense color with your prayer *thought-form*. Simply allow the color or colors to come into your mind. Give yourself time. Once you've identified color, allow it to surround the area of your body you've also identified. Let the energetic sense of your prayer grow into your awareness. Think of your words as energy.

Now, visualize your prayer surrounded with golden white light. Allow it to rise upward in your body and with and outward breath, let it release out of the top of your head, the crown center in your body. Stay with the prayer visually as it moves outward to the universe…surrounded in golden light. Give thanks for its being received in the light. Now universal energy is able to fully work with it.

A Prayer for Times of Resistance

God,
Please help me to keep my mind open to possibility.
Please lift my fears from past events so that they don't control my choices for the future.
Please see my open hands, my open heart. Allow me to stay soft and yielding to the tides,
the flows of this life...even when I feel bad.
Help me to feel your Presence carrying me through.
I need to feel your Presence within me now more than ever.
Please help me to communicate better with other people.
Help me to be a better listener...to truly hear what others are saying.
Please offer me questions to ask when I feel unsure or afraid,
so I don't block my own growth or pathway in this life.
Offer me the grace to apologize if I have unintentionally wronged anyone.
Please send your grace to those I have not been able to reach in my loving,
although I may not know the reasons why right now.
Let your grace be full,
to cover the pain on all sides.
I release and forgive all others from the clouds of pain, fear, and confusion.
I forgive myself and others in my life for our human errors.
Thank you, God, for hearing my prayers.
I now choose to go free with your love and guidance.
Om. Peace. Amen.

Come walk with me, shadow.
Where are we?
Hurt, despair, fear...
All the things I dread most...
And yet when you visit me
I am lead just there...
where I cannot hush the voices in my head
of fear, anger, control, and desire...
You help me to embrace these deep within my being, too.

Chapter Ten

Embracing Shadow

The *shadow* aspect of ourselves is comprised of all the unhealed parts of self that show up within our consciousness to be loved, to be healed. Meeting a difficulty or sense of discord in our minds, where we *could* readily move through it but seemingly can't, is otherwise known as coming face to face with the shadow aspect of our personality. We may try to let our upset go, but find that it is not releasing. It may release to some degree, but if it is not released *completely* it may go for a time, only to revisit us shortly thereafter.

Know that as we walk in the light of Spirit it is completely natural to experience ebbs and flows of awareness. Indeed, a full experience of ourselves involves accepting all aspects of what it is to be *alive* here on earth. Our lives flow in the rhythm of duality, or expansion and contraction within a positive and negative polarity. If we cannot embrace to ourselves the aspect that contracts in response to negative polarity, then we are not honoring *the all* of our being in existence fully here.

We *are* in physical limitation at times; we *are* constantly dealing with the mental aspect of ourselves. Our minds are moving through all kinds of fixation and struggle to hold onto control. Experiencing unconditional love is the ability to love the all of ourselves *and* others—including our shadow.

If we don't yet have it, we can gain the ability to walk through the parts of ourselves that feel unloving and unloved; the part that judges and condemns others' behavior. Yet to think that this shadow element within us can be quickly vanquished would be unrealistic.

Helping ourselves through difficult moods and downswings in our lives goes back to the theory that life is always in process. Life unfolds, and we unfold into who we are more deeply along with it, but we must make the consistent effort to remain conscious, which requires moving through our entire range of feelings.

In dealing with shadow, we will want to walk ourselves through the growth process even more attentively and carefully than we ordinarily do. Shadow aspect cries out for forgiveness, correction of perception, and a warm embrace of self. Meeting and getting to know our shadow side is a very deep part of inner growth. We can grow to know and accept it if we can see that it is there as our teacher, and there also because of the very nature of living in duality, which is the mass energy *thought-form* of this earth, the stage of thinking from which almost everyone formulates thought.

As we reach towards fulfillment, we may feel tugs from our minds about how we may have "failed" at a job, a relationship, a decision-making process, or whatever may be. Think about it…

If life is always in motion, and we have been flowing in it effectively and becoming more aware, we will see that there is no sense of failure, because everywhere we've been and all we have done has been a learning experience. We don't get from *Point A* to *Point C* without going through *Point B*. *Point B* may have felt painful, but we have become stronger inwardly and more understanding for that experience. We can say, when it's over, "I did walk through it, and I will let myself feel my strength and integrity for having done it."

As we are able to know ourselves more fully—in alignment with all our experiences, both seemingly paradoxical or positive—we open to the knowledge of God loving us fully, without judging what brought us here to today or letting it affect the love that we are today.

Many can take on a sense of strength by running forward in this life, tackling work projects and personal issues or constantly learning through intensive study. It is an inherent gift to be able to strive outwardly this way throughout life.

We need to recognize, also, that when we experience life fully and consciously, by staying with its flow and honoring all that occurs as learning-perhaps sometimes having to sort out the pieces as we go—we are being grounded into living a life that is solid. We are feeling and being in *all* of life—both in action and in awareness of Spirit. The more we are fully conscious, the more we will know that these two states are as one. Only our minds, fear, and our own running hides us from this truth.

Understanding and accepting our shadow aspect is part of deep inner growth. As we grow to know shadow, its looming, menacing hold over our lives shrinks. In times of difficulty, we often see that, no matter how great the difficulty, with shadow's emergence we can work with it more closely. The reward also comes in honoring ourselves more fully.

Where a shadow trait is recognized, we can work at learning from it and shifting from its *repetition compulsion* within us. We can also learn patience and respect for ourselves when confronting its difficulty in our lives. The following are some examples of familiar and common *shadow aspects* of the subpersonality, with tips for moving past them:

Blocked Emotions

Blocked emotion intensifies a sense of isolation, a shadow experience. Fear, anger, rage, sadness, and hostility need a space to breathe so that they do not grip us like a vice. Give yourself permission to feel an emotion when you recognize it surfacing. Buried emotions can be hard to recognize and feel as they surface.

When you allow the feeling, this does not mean it will activate immediately in expression. You are simply making a pathway for it to travel by acknowledging it; for example, by saying, "I feel really sad." When the emotion does release, if it appears in tears, shouts, or laughter, let it all through! In a quiet space that is yours alone or with someone you trust, it will come up naturally, as it was meant for you. Do not push yourself to feel it. You will see yourself meeting yourself more deeply as you let your feelings surface. Letting feelings through is a definitive way to care for yourself and to honor yourself more deeply.

A Simple Truth

Sometimes a song or a movie or just hugging a pillow can bring up emotions that are blocked and give them a positive outlet.

As children we are taught to shield hurt at all costs. Think of how healthy patterns of growth would sprout if we were taught *instead* that hurt is real, to experience it and move on without shielding our hurt, knowing ultimately that we are safe and accepted.

Yet life is not a storybook fairy tale. Thinking it should be a certain way, we can limit the energy of the present tense. Through reality lessons, our experiences become more real to us as living foundations, keys to understanding who we are... When this happens, life moves beyond the wish for a fairy tale and into an actual experience based on the deepest love we can ever imagine.

Self-Deception and Judgment

When we find there is an internal argument in our minds, we can know we are not letting ourselves feel the light that is our sense of oneness with all. An argument or a firmly held opinion will not gift us with new energy or insight. If we let our arguments or opinions go, we will not be overtaken by anything negative or controlling. We will find there is a new space to breathe, to make a choice about a new way to see. It is in cutting through deception that we come to a new understanding of the space that is there for us.

Life is not about the *specialness* we long to create, situations that are unique to ourselves alone. Our gift is in realizing that in all things the "whole" of life is the specialness. It is we who, in our sense of limitation, have been confused about the goal. This truth is the clarion call of all that we are, ringing through to us as we are able to receive it.

What would it be like to come to know how wondrous each of us truly is…along with everyone that we know? There is no lack of or shortage of love in this life. We must only become conscious of the love that is always there for us.

A Simple Truth

*If I am holding myself in a place of separation from others, I am not growing in the light.
I need to see or sense the light in others and to expose myself to this; then I will grow again where my seeds have been planted…yielding true love.*

The pain of feeling separate is much more difficult than that which springs from the growth work, but we stay with the former pain or struggle because it is what we know. We cannot always escape the negative that finds us, but we can choose to let it wash through us, to not give it more credence than any other thing in our lives.

It is easy to overlook basic signals in our lives—signals to be alert, to search out, to seek balance, to enliven our souls. When we overlook the signals, it is a message that we are overlooking ourselves. Truly, the scenery we see before us with our eyes is a direct reflection of our inner landscape.

I can sit back and judge people for who they are or for what I think they've done to me. I am shown today that the only thing that sets me apart from them is my actions, and those are what counts. When I criticize, can I say that my actions are different from theirs? We are all made up of the humbling actions that make us human. To walk in action beyond what traps others in this life is to become a teacher by example. To show forth this difference means that God has called us out. It is a calling to move out past the pain of the judgment that binds.

Holding on to Regrets

Holding on to the past and to things we wish we had done differently is literally a waste of our energy in the now. As we look back on the past, we may see things that were troubling and notice that we acted in ways we would not again.

But it is possible to heal the memories of the past. When we do this, what we are healing is the *thought-forms*, because that is what is real to us now, not the actual memories. Memories can hold no real energy in the now; it is only our feelings about them that hold positive or negative energy. So, how can we alter a thought-form?

If a troubling memory comes up for you in your mind, simply revisit it. Let yourself back up mentally to really see images of specific things you were doing at that time. Now notice the slant you are giving it in your mind. Back up even further mentally and tell yourself, "I am going to shift the perspective I have about this into new energy."

Take a minute to sit with the person that you were at that time. What were the things you were struggling with? Were you trying to improve your life at the time? Let yourself see how hard you were trying with that particular lesson. Allow yourself to see how carefully you were walking through your life learning that lesson or teaching, no matter what the outcome ended up being. Stay with who you are in the present, and let the person you are now go back and fully reach out in compassion to how you were being then. Remember, it is not easy to embrace deeper lessons in this life. Sometimes learning has to happen through difficult experiences.

Finally, look at the person you were being then and sense how full your love-energy was, and is today. Today, appreciate that you were moving through a teaching, and that you were absolutely doing your best with the information you had at that time. Okay, maybe you needed to feel a few more bumps and bruises before the lesson was realized, but know that the love that you are never left you. You did the best that you could at that time.

Sometimes fear overtakes our lives and we feel overwhelmed, confused, and unaware of the personal choices that aren't best for us. Today, we can look at the past and *be with* the true peace of mind that we learned through that teaching.

Resentment and Jealousy

When we don't feed ourselves with healthy thoughts about our lives or we overtax our schedules with too many committments, we create pockets of *energy depletion*. When we feel depleted in our lives, we move into feelings of resentment because we are in the place of "without." The sense of "without" is the sense of lack in our lives, and it is what we are used to feeling. In this state of mind it is very common to feel greed, envy, jealousy, and resentment because we are not resting in the serenity that life can provide us with what we need. Here, we need to connect more fully with Spirit because Spirit is the most completely sustaining, ever renewing energy on the planet.

In resentment or other base emotions that can't fuel us, we need to first stop blaming other people or conditions for our pain. Problems are created in our continued learning and successful search for solutions. This is all part of the interplay of life. It is part of being alive and interacting with others on so many different levels. The difficulty with base emotions is not that they are evil, but that they have no fortifying energy in them because they do not stem from the love-energy that is all-sustaining within.

There is nothing wrong with offering correction to ourselves when we find ourselves going off on an emotional tangent from a "without" place. We all forget that our lives can be driven by the loving constant of Spirit.

A Simple Truth

Recognize how many things in this life can distract and confuse a serene space within ourselves. Correction is taking the action of assisting yourself to remember love within you without a sense of failure or punishment for forgetting.

Resentments are a way of alerting us that we have forgotten our fullest resource. They will show up strongly around the hidden corners in our lives. Sometimes they will be with us for a time before we even recognize they are there! How can we deal with them?

One way to clear heavier emotions is to ask for assistance at the end of each day. Just speak to the energies of God, saying, "I ask that anything that came up within me today that was not highest and best for my state of pure being be offered up to the Light to be taken from me and returned to its pure state."

Lack of Boundaries

Living in this life involves navigating various layers of energy and intensities of light-energy…communing beyond that which we see with our eyes. When we are tangling with energies that are not similar to our own wavelength of energy, we may get caught up in difficulty. Without even knowing it, people swap the energies around their physical bodies all the time. Why? Because they have not set healthy boundaries. The extremes of having done this repeatedly and unconsciously are exhaustion, confusion, depression, or a sense of withdrawing.

In maintaining constant, clear boundaries with those around us, we allow ourselves and others a space of awareness of their own growth patterns. We all need to feel a sense of our physical space—and the energetic space around our bodies that is also a part of us. Having solid boundaries in our lives is a constant we hold with others. It is an upholding of self-love and it keeps us from harboring resentments. People are constantly wrestling with the issue of control in one form or another, as a form of imagined safety.

When someone steps into your sense of space, whether physically, mentally, or emotionally, without invitation, they have crossed over a healthy energetic boundary. If you don't recognize this *fully*, part of you will, and you may say or do things you don't mean in an attempt to rebalance your space. The energetic space around you is needed because it houses your capacity to act and your right to grow. You can maintain healthy boundaries by communicating clearly with others what your personal boundaries are and affirming inwardly the decisions you have made about who you are.

Sometimes a person will step across your *energy boundary* because they feel threatened by your growth. They may sense an element of you that is well developed, yet may be lacking in themselves, and they don't know how to build it for themselves from within. So, they reach out and try to "borrow" your energy in this area.

By having *constant, clear* boundaries with those around us, we allow ourselves and others space to gain awareness of their own growth patterns. We may be consciously aware spiritually, but this does not mean that all people are, nor does it mean that we own that "consciousness" by deciding a right or wrong for ourselves or others. Instead, we recognize that God-awareness is a grace that runs through everyone's life, whether they are conscious of it or not. The guidance of God handles and works with each person uniquely and perfectly.

Boundaries keep our pathway clear so we can continue to grow and assist others to do the same. The work of creating boundaries ultimately creates deeper sharing because it allows each of us to know who we are more fully, and that gives us more confidence to reach out in honesty to others.

Anger and Attack

An expression of anger emanates out of us from a feeling of fearfulness or a sense of threat. Though our reservoir of all that we are is constantly enriched with what we need to keep us thriving and happy, due to outer circumstances we don't always remember that. Striking balance in our lives keeps our emotional reservoir full so that anger generally does not become an issue. But when we've gone out of balance, it can emerge with a fury!

Still, we alone must be responsible for maintaining balance and fullness in our own reservoir. This means being conscious of those times when we are losing our balance—before fear turns into full blown anger! Losing balance can happen in a flash, and it most often happens in the midst of our communications with each other.

If we feel like something gets drained from our reservoir out of nowhere, perhaps by an action or statement from someone else that is upsetting, we get angry. If we are uncomfortable with feeling anger, it will bubble up in different ways. We may feel it as physical tension, a clenched jaw, a headache, a sore muscle, or achy, tense shoulders. Another way we experience anger is in our own severe judgment of other people.

Being able to hear ourselves judging others is a big step towards self-nurture. Somewhere in our minds, we all judge! But the mind moves to be in a place of safety. When it feels its safety is threatened, it will lash out in attack thoughts, attempting to regain a sense of control.

An opinion sent our way from someone else may anger us because we sense part of our freedom to think our own thoughts being taken away. See an opinion for just what it is-no more, no less. Opinions offered to us or from us usually come from wanting something more. Wanting something more is an illusion…because all that there is is available to us at all times.

The love is all within us, just waiting to be discovered. Anger and attack are signs that we are not getting something that we need at that moment. The trouble is that we push and pull at our outer life (and anyone in it!) to give us what we want to make us happy, but the joys of happiness cannot last within or feed us when we are carrying deep wounds at our center. There is then no meeting place within us for happiness to go. It is diffused or repelled; then we grab for something different, sometimes injuring ourselves deeply.

We all have wounds of varying degrees hidden in the closets of our past. Working on uncovering them and understanding them or getting help to do so is substantially assisting, but seeing the problem is still not enough to completely shift body, mind, and soul. From these wounds, a remembrance must sprout. It is the remembrance of the self as love that has the power to heal.

A Simple Truth

True healing begins when we can look within at our own shadow, knowing we are always given a new day to move forward and that tomorrow will provide us with new insights and assistance to make shifts and changes, should we choose to do so...

How can we deal with unwanted anger? We can embrace responsibility for our actions and how they have impacted others. We can shift our internal sight and own responsibility for our habits and addictions and how they have impacted others. We can allow a shift in sight to change our actions with others in our lives, and also to change patterns of behaviors with them. As we open up more to love, anger will be neutralized.

Fear and Addiction

Remember that fear springs from the mind. It comes up in many ways to block growth. Judgment is the hammer that drives the fear home. Judgment is a decision that has been made. Do you hear the door slamming? What purpose does it serve to quickly shut the door? It may initially feel safer, but the only real safety is knowing that there is nothing to fear.

Absolute freedom starts with moving out of the torturous repetition of the mind. The mind judges, condemns, and decides. Why? Because it holds fear. And fear can only confuse, because it does not want to release power. One who is walking the pathway of Spirit cannot partner with fear or he/she will find himself fixated in the mind—the true self held hostage by ego's fearful conclusions.

The shadow self plays off addictions and compulsions because they hold us in a blinding sense of separateness and aloneness. In addiction, the mind, heart, body, and soul are trapped in isolation. Our fears can drive us into addiction, and fear keeps us there. It is a place of complete *unnaturalness* within our bodies, and it is an escape from the emotional pain that we are afraid to feel or work through.

We use patterns of compulsive behavior (for example alcohol or food addiction, smoking, gambling, shopping, sex or love addiction—even being addicted to our emotions) to run away from ourselves and, in the process, we bury *all* of our senses. The addictive mind strives to arrive at a false sense of safety and the action of escape is the route the mind sees to accomplish this.

The energy of addiction floats in the ethers of our lives, just above us, waiting to attach. It attaches to our imbalances. It attaches to our egos when we focus on perfection or think we have to have all the answers. When life feels confusing, weird, or ugly and all wrong…it could be an addictive thought pattern rearing its head again. In this our mind can't help us and the sense of our heart will seem lost or missing.

When an addiction tape plays in the mind, it is one fragment of the mind hunting around to find false satisfaction. The whole body, mind and soul does not feel intact that way. It is not the true reality. The true reality is changeless. It is the recognition of the love that you are.

Twelve Step work encourages the surrender of this mindset to a "Higher Power," so the addiction is out of the way of the process of inner healing. Without spiritual surrender, the addictive mindset may have to be surrendered many times, because the mind and body *will* try relentlessly to take back control.

Judging an addiction or habit as *bad* further reinforces a sense of shame and a desire for escape. We may feel that addictions are "bad" because they can overrun our lives. Sometimes addictions go very far in their damage to the manageability of our lives before we are motivated at all to get the help we need. Further, addiction alienates us from understanding the pain we keep trying to cover up. Understanding that we have pain is the first step in healing the trigger points of addiction. Rather than condemning, try the following approach.

Be forgiving to yourself by recognizing that you picked up an addiction to try to help yourself from the emotional pain or lack of resolve that you felt. To just sit with what you are trying to avoid in your emotional self, without judging, brings about an understanding that says something like, "Well, this situation just is what it is." In saying this, you have the opportunity to come back to yourself and to be present to yourself in all the feelings that arise. When you can acknowledge your buried feelings, you are in a better position to come up with viable solutions to the problems they may be creating.

In working through addictive behavior, if the feelings are very difficult, give yourself the space and time you need to let them surface. It is critical to the full expression of your strength of character to work with your feelings, because the wake of unhealed addiction can leave you unable to love or care for yourself or to reach out in true *soul level caring* for or giving toward others from the heart.

Taking Responsibility

Without taking responsibility, we feel ourselves to be victims of the circumstances of this life. In truth, it is we who are not standing up in action for what is right for ourselves. When we choose to take the part of the victim, we blame others for the situations in which we find ourselves.

Responsibility is the living action of showing up for ourselves, for our lives, and for all those we are close to, so that we don't fall into the *victim trap*, which only hurts both ourselves and those around us. Taking full responsibility for our lives involves showing up with our hearts as well as our logical minds. Our hearts give love-energy to our bodies, yet we can easily walk around only half plugged into what we are doing because our minds are jumping around in fear through past and future tenses.

The challenge of living fully is showing up with our heart exposed, not because we have overcome vulnerability, but because we have opened our hearts enough to really show up to feel the experience of living more completely. From a loving space within, we take the time we need to choose *what's right for us* in this life and to honor the choices of others, as well.

Mind, body, and Spirit-awareness asks us to take responsibility for our lives so that we can stay balanced and live in that mode from a place of integrity and strength. Gaining a true sense of inner responsibility in our decision to be conscious is a direct gift and blessing from Spirit.

If we are doing our best to be responsible for our own lives, then we also need to not interfere with anyone else taking responsibility for theirs. If we are in another's point of responsibility, we are interfering with God's gift-giving. The deepest gift you can give another is to allow them their emotional freedom by freeing them from your control or opinion. Now the work of Spirit can begin directly with that person, and because you had the strength to walk away energetically you extended the hand of compassion, of unconditional love. This placed the person directly in the hands of God's assistance, and God knows the best ordering out for each person's life more than any of us can presume to know. The more we can be responsible for our own life and true, Divine essence, the more others will also sense our love for them, because we will be truly and fully present, not just going through the motions of life, distracted and unhappy.

If we take responsibility to live consciously, we will gain confidence that we are handling our lives from the highest Light, and choices will be clear and understandable in ways they may never before have been.

A Glimpse into the Underworld

Figuratively speaking, the underworld is a space where the unconscious mind rises to the forefront through our shadow aspect. It is this *acting out of shadow* aspect of ourselves, to the point where it is a different way of existing in the world, which we call *the underworld*. Chronic addiction, being in compromised relationships, having affairs, living in fantasy, obsessive thinking—all fit in the category of underworld actions. This is a condition that we slip into when life becomes overwhelmingly unbearable, where we lose the willingness to stay with responsibility in this life.

Underworld actions usually stem from the origins of low self-esteem and lack of motivation to get help for ourselves in addressing the source of our pain. (Physical or mental disorders or imbalances are not a part of the underworld that is described here.)

When we catch ourselves experiencing glimpses of the underworld in our own lives, we know that we are being waved a warning flag. We have been put in the fast lane of our learning curve. Still, slipping into an unconscious way of living can be insidious, and no one is completely immune to it. A temporary feeling of escape can derail us and turn into months or even years of rebuilding in order to find inner balance again.

When we see others slip into underworld behavior, we can know that their sight is not clear. We can offer support and love their way, but they may not have the capacity to accept it. Sometimes we must accept that this is their choice. They choose to undergo this series of learning experiences in this life. Your work is to release that choice to Spirit for assistance. God-light will find its way into that person's life when and as it is meant to…so that they may truly know truth and be guided along their own pathway to growth.

When we cry out
the deepest to God in prayer
for love to be found in our life
in partnership with another,
and we are open and listening...
God will tell us
That the love we are seeking
is found in its entirety within.

The fathomless love we
are seeking "out there,"
will first be found within.
It is a sacred marriage of our soul
to our embodiment here.

It is the communion of
walking a sweet mystery
where new is found again and again,
and, as we feel newness created within,
we are gifted to see the world
and all those in it in this way...
so we walk in reverence
of our new sight,
that we may be able to
give in its service,
its mystery...
and know more deeply who we are.
No attachment...
Part of a vast, transcendent whole.

Chapter Eleven

Loving for Life: The Mystery of Higher Love

Higher Love is the well known whistler in the hills of many gardens—both the face of seeking and the face of love. The whistler does not come to the crowd and point you out as one who has chosen to follow His song. No, He makes his song hauntingly beautiful, hidden in the soft curves of the rolling, velvet hills. You search and reach to find Him in every peak you run to ascend; in every calico hill you tumble down, creating and living life's challenges as you go!

Still, He waits—the silhouette of a piper, flute in hand, and if you find Him and run towards Him, telling Him you are ready to solve the mystery of love, you will be waiting in silence with Him on that hill for a long time. Maybe Higher Love, in its trembling tenderness, will find you—but only when you've marched through the foothills of desire.

It is truth that as we seek to know of God within more fully, we move into alignment with Higher Love. Higher Love evolves past what we have known of our concept of love. It is the actual, deep experience that we can start to feel in living moment to moment in the truth of the love that we are.

The key word to grasping Higher Love is to know that it springs from what we know as "feeling" in our emotional body, and it expands out from there to encompass a deeper resource of love within our pure hearts. We call Higher Love a mystery because it is always unfolding before us in representation of what we experience as love within. It moves past being sought out in an agenda or sequence of events.

Because the face of God is ever-flowing and ever-creating, knowing its presence within is knowing Higher Love. There is nothing to do but to "be" in this love. Staying out of definition is staying with the fluidity of the mystery.

The veils of illusion that we live in are what crush the sense of Higher Love in our lives. When we project outward in fear or contraction, we inhibit our ability to flow with this love. We move past pulling at love and in our walking in trust we sense the greater availability of Higher Love. It is gifted as we keep our hearts open to receive it. When we flow with it in trust, we experience sublime happiness felt in the heart. We feel peace, and we come to know that miracles can be daily occurrences, especially in our interactions with others.

We have so often ascribed the meaning of "love" as love shared with another. Romantic love is as intense as emotion will ever get. There is no feeling quite like it, and once we have a taste of it, we will have the urge to reclaim it in our lives. Romanticism is merely one facet of love. Feeling magnetic attraction to another is an energy that connects directly to the body, so it is ultimately finite in its expression.

Sexual attraction is connected to romantic love because it rests on desire and the fulfillment of desire. The combination of chemistry and romantic longing can keep a relationship alive for many years, but sooner or later one's conscious self comes face to face with one's subconscious self, even in relationship. This is where relationship trouble can start. We see the incongruence between who we are and how we are behaving in the relationship. Sometimes we make unnecessarily big compromises just to keep a relationship alive.

Divine or Higher Love is directed through us; through our heart's expression from the one everlasting source of Spirit, so it knows no bounds. The mind has trouble with describing or assimilating this, but Higher Love remains within us always, and when it touches our consciousness we experience it as a mystery. When we can let go and trust in the mystery as it unfolds, it becomes a beautiful dance of discovery.

We often associate letting go or releasing as painful or sad, but to let Higher Love into our lives the most fully, we are in a process of letting go many times, and as we let go, we actually feel how this love has found us.

A Simple Truth

We start to know that we hold the key to full love deep within our hearts as we accept that the process of seeking is our responsive answer to Love's calling. It is in the process of seeking to know we are found by God in love, and there is no one formula. Being found is infinitely individual, though it occurs millions of times over.

The energy of Higher Love as it unfolds is quiet and subtle, yet paradoxically it fuels us to move ever onward to seek it once we have recognized its flow. When we walk living this sacred mystery with another, we are in deep, everlasting communion with all of life…*with God*. We reverently seek to know more deeply of the divinity in one another, and this action of mindfulness transmits grace and a very fine beauty, one that extends far beyond the physical body yet weaves through it in a symphony of expression.

The greatest gift we can give ourselves is to let the mystery be the mystery. For example, think of gazing into a mirror which at first appears hazy. The haziness represents the vision that shifts as we move to know ourselves in connection to others in our lives. The mystery of Higher Love is the journey of moving into the mists of the mirror. Higher Love is the vision of love in purity beyond the mist, but it moves through the mist to call us to seek the clarity of itself.

Each time we are graced with clear knowing from God because we sought it, we will recognize it as love we see in each other and in all living things. We are all sacred mirrors to each other, and a deepening of love's calling will always be placed before us as long as we are alive. It is the truth of our journey here on earth. Every single person we communicate with is a living opportunity for us to know ourselves more fully.

That is why communication is vitally important (and why extreme isolation and separation from others can put us out of balance.) At first, we might hesitate to seek Divine love, feeling that we will have to give up what we have held onto so tightly in our definition of love. It is an absolute truth that as you move into the mystery of this Higher Love, you experience blessing beyond measure. You begin to know deeply that in the flow of this you are receiving and bathing in a sense of love that is with you always.

Nothing can be lost to you in the experience of Higher Love, but you cannot simply sit back and wait to receive it. Seek to know it by seeking often to recognize love in yourself and in others.

Usually when we look in the mirror, we focus on particulars that we are used to seeing within ourselves. Try the following exercise to catch a glimpse of divinity in the moment.

Mirror Exercise

Stand with your face a foot or so back from a mirror... with soft lighting or daylight in the room. Focus on looking into your eyes, without judgment. Notice their color and their softness...the eyebrows and eyelashes. Whenever you feel a harsh thought, let your glance soften and take in your whole face. Remember... just tell yourself, "No judgment."

As you look at your whole face through the eyes of love, feel yourself accepting your skin. Let yourself see how soft it is. You may start to see, as you continue to look, that it is luminous...that it has a slight golden glow which rises at the surface. This is the expression of love in your face. Let yourself love the timeless quality of your face and its pure expression, beyond the narrow scope of what you are used to seeing. Smile at yourself as you are able, for your willingness to be present and to witness your own Divinity shining forth. Know in this exercise that you are allowing yourself to be graced with vision. You will feel the blessing. You may experience a shift or awakening within your consciousness.

Higher Love in Relationship

The real aspect of relationship of connection to another resides in the heart. In a spiritually based relationship, all the musings of the mind won't deepen the connection. You must go to the heart, where you find the truth of all that you are. The truth is so simple, so pure, so true, that the mind's arguments can sweep over it to drown it out. The ways in the mind are endless, but to the heart it's all truth beyond words.

A Simple Truth

*When Divinity comes knocking,
one cannot wait too long.
It is natural and becomes even moreso with
each breath of love-awareness.
At the highest level of heart initiation,
want-agenda cannot be present.
It must be released and cast aside.*

In long-term conscious relationship there is a stronger spiritual thread that can be grown between two people that outlasts romantic love and enhances the connection profoundly. Relating to one another from the place of Higher Love invites further adventure and passion into the essence of being alive. The core elements to Higher Love in a conscious relationship are that there is minimal fear present through the bridge of trust and consequently there is a natural draw to want to express and share. Where trust is present, honesty is alive and vital in communication.

We can only know another person to the degree that they know and love themselves, because that is the degree to which they can open to us. Also, the reverse is true. We will only open up to love to the degree that we know love within our own selves. When Higher Love graces a relationship, it is because two people are fully capable of realizing the love within themselves as complete. It is complete love—all encompassing and ever-freeing.

The old foundation of love within us came from the outgrowths of strong feelings of romantic love or longing. These feelings had sounded, "I want" or "I need," with increasing desire. So many of us have been used to these feelings as the norm in our expression of love. Now without doing all that want—feeling, where would that love be within us?

All the wanting that we feel in love patterns we've known comes from a sense of separation; a sense of lack within. It is an illusion. The self must be accepted by the love powered source on all levels of what it projects and mirrors back to: the soul. The soul knows how to love (it always has known), for it needs no forgiveness, such as the self does. It is pure. It is free.

We want ownership of romantic love so that we can feel safe, but when we can allow the feelings to exist freely within us we will know that we are creating a new sight for ourselves. It is a pure sight that offers much (when you allow love to free float—not attaching—within you). Now you will start to sense the free-floating nature of it into all the spaces around you and within others. You will see that it is abundant, and that you don't have to trap it for your own mind assimilation because it is the air you breathe. It is all of creation. You do not *possess* anything.

Then, "What do we possess? *What is ours?"* we want to know. Ours is the sense that we have of ourselves in relationship to this Divine flow. All Spirit is gently coaxing us to do is to hold our "selves," our conscious physical being, in soul alignment to this love-awareness by letting it *be* in its mystery.

Being in love…in recognized free float…is our space to breathe with who we truly are, our expanded self, our *I Am* presence. In this love, we are able to give ourselves a real sense of being here, which is a constant in duality. This is further enhanced by accepting that, "Yes, my physical body is finite, but this deeper awareness of my infinite soul is birthing in me, and I need do nothing but feel its love."

Riding the mystery of love in relationship is staying committed to be in the Spirit rhythm that is present beyond the pull of the mind, to stay connected to the greater awareness that is truth. Think for a moment about the following mysteries of truth in relationships.

Truths for Relationships

· Love is love represented in action. Represent outwardly the truth that you are.
· Anger and sadness are not who you are; they are simply facets of expression.
· Uncovering truth in difficulty leads to deeper expression of beauty.
· The heart will help you express compassion when you let it in.

· The relationship is not a dress rehearsal. Be willing to show up fully in the moment with each other. Listen and reach out in love.
· Commitment, faith and trust are sacred gifts that create a safe space to express love toward one another in its fullest sense.

Love is the soul's expression of pure beauty. It does not fixate on conditions or objects. It is simply the space of being in the heart. Consider the following word picture as you seek to understand this truth:

To ride the tides of relationship to their full season, one must be fully *seen*...to one's full potential. It is not fair for me to offer my hand and then pull it away. I cannot offer my hand unless I know, in my fullness, its worth. Then when I offer it to you from the love of my heart, you can know it is a strong hand—extended in the light of faith and trust, enshrouded with rainbow after rainbow of love-light. These hands, they will go the distance. Exquisite joy and sublime beauty is the offering of these hands...

A Simple Truth

The hands represent the extending outward in love offering. This is, in essence, moving from the heart. So much energy can be redirected if we align with love in action. When you feel love, show it, but do not attach to outcome. If you feel unsure of another's love, ask them about it and hear their truth.

We are a part of this vaster love, and the way that we live the love is by honoring its mystery...and acknowledge its strength-stronger than any healing force we've known! First, we acknowledge our search for love; then we give ourselves permission to open to its mystery.

A Prayer to the Mystery

God,
I open to the sweet mystery within me.
All the open spaces there within,
waiting to create into expression,
into form.

I know you hold the wisdom
of the blueprint.

I know I hold the candle
that I may better see it
in my willingness, my truth,
my strength, and my courage
to seek.
And while I can accept all the forces
that be,
Help me in these moments
to part the waters.
Back wind!
Back water!
Back fire and earth....
into the empty spaces. God, move them
into the no-thingness.
Shape me in the mystery
that I may come to be
my destiny in this life.

Om. Peace. Amen.

*There is a space
that breathes, that is home,
and in this space
we don't need to be
right or wrong;
We are ourselves,
and we invite others in from this place.*

*We breathe in safety
because we were all created by God
and in this
we share our likeness.*

*We can look out
from the eyes of love—
no matter the circumstance,
no matter the weather...
let me offer you
the kindness of my heart
from my hands extended,
I help you and you help me;
You can breathe here, and so can I.*

*From this space
there is room to touch down
into deeper and deeper
realms of love...and into life.*

Chapter Twelve

Compassionate Love

Compassionate love is the expression of Higher Love which we grace out into the world through action. It births in us as we live the middle ground of mindful and responsible living—fair, true and wondrously sustaining, reaching out to one another unconditionally in the spaces of full love.

Where there is a need for global healing, we will sense a need for a love that can connect us to a sense of oneness beyond the complexities of holding ourselves in a sense of separation. Compassionate love is the answer to the calling today for a love that can heal us all, spanning out to connect us one by one.

Compassion, graced through honoring Higher Love within us, also moves out into the world from the energy of the heart. It is more than a mentally driven expression. It involves all parts of us; physical, mental, emotional and spiritual… showing up in a given situation to offer loving action or thoughts. The mind becomes motivated through this offering of love straight from the heart. It also becomes a witness to our ability to make a difference in the world, no matter how large or how small.

We are all unique in our personalities' representation in this life, but through reaching out in compassionate love we can remember just how connected we really are.

Compassionate love extended plays music to our hearts. It is the hand extended in assistance to another in a time of need. It is reaching out in prayer to family or strangers in times of crisis. It is holding the door for someone, or letting someone have your rightful parking space. It is reaching out to comfort another through being present in pain that is difficult to witness.

Each interaction with another, no matter who it is, is a call into loving action. You offer this love from a feeling of centeredness and strength inside of you, and the gift of purity emanating from the heart extends to the other from this space.

Only fear holds back compassionate love. Fear exists in a place of separation and lack. Sometimes we have to work steadfastly to not become hardened in our ways and opinions around others. The task is to soften our sense of indifference, to feel our true place within interactions with others.

A Simple Truth

No one hangs on successfully to a new reality of love in the face of doubt. In all situations, Divine and compassionate love Is the face of security.

Compassionate love is the wellspring of love beyond fear. It moves forward in the fullness that comes from the fuel of Spirit. It exists in the spaces of *"I love"* and *"I Am the love."* Truth is met in this "right" action that is *"God-action."* In God-action, you know nothing. In God-action, you are moved through, and your movement is pure love through compassion. To embody this love, fear cannot be present.

You will recognize when you are offering compassionate love, because of the warm and peaceful feelings that return to you. As you experience compassionate giving, you will draw more authentic experiences of love to yourself, arising out of the natural flow of unconditional love. This is truly living from the heart.

More and more, God will move you to want to be that

expression of love. You will be guided naturally, but you will need to let go of your old concepts of love. We recognize the old concepts of love as we sense the conditions we may have placed on it. For example, wanting to give for the thought of getting something back...or holding back our love because we feared rejection. The pushing and pulling actions of relationship must be released in order to experience compassionate love. As we can be in states of surrender and let go, we begin to understand that the deeper layers of God-connected love are graced to us.

When we live in the heart, we extend out in honesty to another from that place. We see with the eyes of beauty. We see faces—people before us that want to feel and connect with love, just as we do. This is the vision—the sight—of compassionate love. Love, ultimately, is all the golden threads of energy that connect us to our remembrance of our connection to God. Connecting with others in compassionate word and deed activates these golden threads that enhance our awareness of Spirit moving through our lives. We start to birth the newness of who we truly are...as one with love out into the world.

We may not initially recognize incorporating compassionate action all the time. It takes time for the tapes of the mind, its original sense of love, to slowly be erased. In fact, it is a real challenge not to take prerecorded ideas with us on the road of true love. The experience is writing itself as it happens, and willingness is its fuel.

Compassionate love is the door we hold open within us, even when we want to shut it the most. The door is the door of our high heart, ever-connected to God. It swings open only with unflinching love—love that knows no argument and exerts no demands. This does not mean we must accept being treated poorly by another, only that we approach each other "eyes wide open," accepting our choices about that door of love.

If I can think of one thing that undoes the sense of separation between myself and another—something I truly love about them unconditionally—we have now moved a step closer to one another in compassion. If I can move past the fear to truly love another person and all that they are, I am giving them a most precious gift. I meet with the all-knowing, the changeless face of love…the sweetest smile…the warmest embrace…loving the Divine in you, loving me reflected back. In the repeated acknowledgement of this flow, wisdom is gifted-wisdom which can be applied to all the living spaces of our lives. This happens as we experience the presence of the Divine within us.

We have the potential to come from the spaces of compassion extending outward in all of our interactions and relationships. First, we have acknowledged that there was much more to the love we felt inside of ourselves. Second, we affirmed that is flowing within us and all around us at all times whether we consciously sense it or not.

To grow compassionate love in our hearts we move with experiences. We open towards them in love. This is the expression of love in action. As we move our love out into the world, God will grace our supply so that we are moving with the love.

We can want certain relationships in our lives with all our heart and soul, but if we have reached this level of a knowing experience with God, we stand on the precipice of understanding…and the precipice will either grace the love forward or hold it back, depending on the action we choose at that moment.

Attachment in love, to outcome or to conditions, cannot be partnered in compassionate love. In the want for love's return, there is a holding on, and the holding on displays the sense I feel that I am somehow separate from the love. Where there is a sense of separation within me, it is a call to my journey of inner healing. To heal my own sense of self, my awareness of who I truly am, I must take the wanting or the person thought it is attached to and allow my vision to become God-vision, meaning that I am able to see, sense, and feel God-energy emanating from this person.

I will not pretend to know what he or she, with their personality or agenda, is really about in the moment. I will just know that beneath their feelings and the way in which they project to the world around them, there is a God reservoir that makes them pure love, and able to be loved as such. When I look at this love and allow myself to sense it, I can see it knows no differentiation. It is an amazing current of love, but the same love I could feel for the country I live in, for a blue sky, for my mother, for my children, and so on. In other words, this compassionate love of God, runs in a constant current *underneath* what we have partitioned love to be.

A Simple Truth

God is everywhere, and at times He grants me the vision to see His love in everything. When I act from this sightedness, I am extending compassionate love.

To be a believer goes deeper than opening your eyes; you must see and hear with the energy of your heart. This is compassionate love and energy flowing within you...*all love*, ever-present. You will not be wasting time and energy trying to explain what the love looks or feels like. Most of this can get lost easily in the translation; the vibration is so finely tuned. Just know that you are representing the love-energy in your actions. You are that love energy.

Part V

Ever Blossoming Out in the World

*To be real
is to be real in action.
All action is
showing up in front of God
With your palms turned up.
In this essence,
you are asking God to guide you within
because external listening alone
feels incomplete.*

*And God will say,
"Yes, I can and will show you...
I'll show you through the living action
we walk through together,
flowing out love.'*

Chapter Thirteen

Being "Real"

What does it mean to be "real?" The word *real* as its used here is to illustrate a level of living we choose. When you are "real" to yourself and your life, you have made a decision to stay with truth in living, which points out to you an awareness that all of life is a learning process of undoing or unfolding that which keeps you from the expression of yourself as truth, as love.

Here we stay centered in our lives and give outward from a place of compassionate love. To do this, we start to know that we must stay connected to the consciousness of heart energy, which says that I Am love and you are love.

You are given a deeper internalized sense of this truth when you no longer feel as strongly swayed by the many tides of this life. There is an absolute state of grace and calm that comes with sight that offers a knowing that, indeed, we are not separate from one another at the level of our soul's interaction.

Truth does not need any explanation. It is just the purest resonance of what you sense is you. Its expression moves all through you, and when you feel it the directions to your life at that time will feel very simple.

We will get to a place in our spiritual journey where we will know that our lives cannot be lived out in the space of reaction to all the external dramas and pressing situations in this life. We cannot escape from the everyday things that make our life here rich and full, on positive and negative levels, but we can move through what we are faced with without having to lose our footing.

We can surrender to the fact that it is impossible for one human being to make right decisions in right timing all of the time. We start to know we can flow with God in living moment to moment, event to event, which is *"real time."* We can observe life patterns and understand that of which we are capable and that of which we are not. We can be compassionate and observant to others and to ourselves, but stay detached so that we can hold a deeper capacity for love in our hearts.

When our minds aren't so bogged down with internal dialogue or dilemma we are free to experience the outward flow of the heart in its expression of love, holding our light in the comings and goings of this life. When you recognize emotion or drama but let it flow through you instead of spending a lot of time and energy trying to get past it or figure it out, then you free your heart to remember its oneness. You are not discounting feeling, emotion, or thought, but you are staying with the recognition that it can flow through you when you let it.

In the flow-through, a healing occurs within your heart. This healing within the heart can occur over and over within you. Each time the heart remembers the love, it naturally moves out in compassionate expression through you. It assists in healing the world of hate, pain, indifference, and prejudices. It is all-encompassing, and it operates through duality at all times in rhythms of contraction and expansion. It heals the suffering in duality always, regardless of what level it is on, because it is stronger than the messages in duality that emanate from conflict in the mind. Try assuming the posture below to gain further freedom and insight on this truth:

How You Can Show up Fully Intact in the Moment

· You are in touch with your boundaries and the needs of your freed child within.
· You have a sense of soul-level awareness at your physical body level. This emanates *soul beauty* expression down to your cells.
· You can feel your freedom to express yourself and your flexibility in changing conditions around you.
· You sense your changeless face of *love expression* that resides more deeply than emotion.

Each of us is a key player within the screenplay of life, and our part is critically needed. When we can know that we can live responsibly within this framework of a greater, truer expression (or picture) of reality, the way will be made clear for us to live this in outward expression.

We all have the capacity to live our vision, the part of us that can hold fast to the picture of keeping our mind and heart open to receive guidance. Conscious interactions lead to processing more deeply in self-inquisition, which can feel very challenging at times. This processing will lead you past what you have known in definition. If you listen to your process and trust Spirit, you will be given the guidance to move through.

One of the keys to walking in the fullest expression of yourself in this life is to accept that God provides us with as many situations as we need at any given time to show us what we are representing in our lives. Each person or interaction is a clear mirror for us, to show the level of truth within us. Incomplete draws incomplete to itself, superficial attracts superficial and so on. In interactions with others, know that both you and the other will absorb truth to the level that you recognize it within. God gifts sight of what's real to love-expression and what is incongruent to it. If we are holding the truth of love within us, what is not congruent to its expression will be recognized, and we are given choice to move past it that we may continue to be in the highest love emanation.

The degree to which I am "real" and feeling "real' both with myself and with others is the amount of love-light, God-energy, that I let in. The amount I let in depends on the amount that I surrender into the process of moment-to-moment living. Sometimes it's the simplest learning and action in this life that feels the most challenging or difficult.

To be awake in this life on levels deeper than you've ever known is to experience challenges in your mind often. I see how true this is in my own life, yet somehow, somewhere, I step through a doorway to this full experience, and everything now is "the real," and in the "real." I do what is asked of me without questioning.

When I am living in the now, fully present with my attention, I can see and know that I am building value in my life from inside of me expressing outward to life. When I focus in the now I live in truth, and truth moves outward to create the highest in my life. At times I am gifted from God, and it feels like it's a confirmation that says, "All is well, you are on the right track."

Here, from a birds-eye view, God shows me a picture of myself, creating playful scenes, dramas, and all the messes that I am reminded that *I create* to move through my learning and my soul's growth. In higher perspective, guidance reminds me there are always smiles, laughter, and reasons to celebrate when learning hurdles are overcome.

*I Am the egg
cracking open.
I Am the shudders before birth.
See how I shudder; then sleep,
then shudder.*

*See how it all glows—
the warmth, the light
to move, to open
the awakening of sight.*

*I Am the Little One
and the Big One, both.*

*I am the seed
and the flower.*

Chapter Fourteen

Fully Creating Outward: Being Love in Walking Action

In this life, under the close guidance of God we will always be given a choice to flow with a current that runs through all of us and through all of our lives. We might call this a *creation current*. In our lives, we are always choosing to flow *with* creation or not to do so. Creation, the energy that moves us to our full potential, is the flow of love infused within us at a cellular level. When we are flowing with it, it is moving us to become love more fully—both within ourselves and in representation in the world.

Love is *love in action*. Words can come from many places within us. Intentions and expectations come from places inside of us, too. They emanate out from mental and emotional levels within, but this is not fully who we are. The creation seed within each one of us comes from *the all* that we are. It does not birth from particulars. It is moving us to be all we are in representation of all we are.

For example, if I set about to prove I can do something, then I am moving forth in an effort to make an effect on my outward surroundings. I am aiming for a desired result, a goal that I would like to reach based on what I desire an outcome to be. I am setting forth to prove or to show something about myself. When I live in representation of the *creation current* of God within me, I am recognizing the truth that I Am this expression of love and that this is the fullest expression from within me.

Expression of love is perfect. It is simple and true. In this truth, it moves way beyond the need for words and formulas or the proof of them in explanation. It is creation—naturally emanating from me as the person I come to represent myself in this world. It is not *propelled* action....it is the action of *being itself,* which creates what is from the highest....beyond what we can know in our minds. It simply *is*.

This does not mean that my life will become dysfunctional because I am not paying attention to its details and looking towards the future. When I have chosen to follow in the creation of God current, inherently knowing that the love within me is the entire sustenance to my life, then I am always moving in highest action with myself and with others. My life starts to naturally represent this in all ways, as long as I do not throw up road blocks in an overpowering need to be right, to understand, or to give in to fear of the unknown. Of course in my journey, many times I will return to questioning and doubt. It is important for me to recognize that the current is a constant. I will not be dropped from it, nor will it ever leave me based on how I am reacting or handling my life.

The willingness to re-seek and re-discover love down all the avenues of awareness of the creation current of God tangibly in one's life as a knowing is a precious gift beyond any measure, but it is not at all out of reach to anyone. The immediate thought or feeling is that it is unseen and out of reach. This illusion exists simply because the creation current can not be explained or described by the mind. It is lived out effortlessly in the willingness to represent love in its trusting action.

When you can sense you are wanting to create in your life from your awareness of the creation current, ask yourself, "Is there a passageway for my creation?" You will sense the answer to this question as a *knowing* within you by the way you feel. If you feel there is a passageway, then your biggest task is only to remove the obstacles that block the fulfillment of its flow to you.

Another example of creation is the difference between how you think of your mind and your personality (i.e. I am witty, punctual, sensitive, and articulate). When you set about to make something happen in your life, you utilize where you feel your strengths are to set your plans into motion. You work hard with yourself to reach goals. This is creation at the mental level, and it is the level most of us operate from in our lives. It is highly functional. We thrive all our lives from this level.

We can see here that the personality level has an amazing ability to create from its strengths. Similarly, we can fall from spaces of mental creativity when we turn on ourselves, or get down on ourselves, feeling we can't accomplish a goal or desire.

The creation current of God is the level beneath mental thought and the planning of making things happen. It is impervious to the whims of the mind. The *creation current* is the fuel within you that has always existed, so it is there before what you think you represent, and because it is so incredibly pure and strong, it generates creation out of the pure essence of love.

My willingness to re-seek and to rediscover this love through all the many rich avenues and roadways I am lead down in my experiences of this life will lead me back to an awareness of the creation current that is within me. My willingness is the golden key that opens the awareness of creation to my consciousness. Each time I rediscover it in my awareness it becomes a stronger lovelight glowing from within me, and as I know it more fully I will create from it more in my true expression to the world. My expression dances with me and I dance with it. It is the celebration of being alive on all levels of awareness, and it seeks itself beneath all the other essential layers that move us through our lives.

True creation energy mimics the times you saw your favorite song performed live…how it moved all through your body…or the dance you feel come alive when you really connect in love to another…or the excitement and anticipation you feel when you step towards a huge challenge. These incredible feelings are able to rise up within you because they are part of the larger Source that fuels them. The more that you can realize this concept, the more creative energy makes itself available to you.

Emotions are finite and move through us in expression. Our thoughts, though they may feel very powerful, are finite too. They move through the mind, and are past. The creation current of love is infinite within us, and it grows within us as we exercise ourselves as love in action. When we are love in action, we are living in co-creation with all of life—the deeper sustenance rhythm of love running under the rhythm of duality. In co-creation, we are taking responsibility to choose to uphold the current within us in right action.

Our normal interactions, activities, and everyday practices in being a seeker touch the creation current. Whether we are out in a quiet spot in nature or feeling a strong connection vibe with someone in a busy shopping mall, at some point the flow of the mainstream of the current will want to unify the connection with a seeker…like the magnetic pull of the tide reaching the shore…

This is the experience of God wanting us to know what we are a greater part of and calling us in the rhythmic waves. When we are riding these waves, we are in the creation current. Life becomes clearer directionally and the love of God is ever-flowing because we are knowing what it feels like to flow in it. We have now established a more constant anchoring in our I Am sense of self.

It is the "one Source" that gifts all into our being, allowing us to be fully present and alive. Here we start to feel birth on all its levels because the present moment we are in is birthing creation all the time—the creation of life, the creation of expression, the expression of love. We do not have to fear shifts because we are moving through them with an infallible source of sustenance that carries us on its vibration.

*God, Who has gifted me my origins
has gifted me the return and the stay.
How do I bask in the
full light of the garden?*

*Where there is sunlight
there will always be moonlight, as well.*

*The current finds you in your flow
and assists you as you go*

*Make yourself ready, then,
for the doorway to serve is opening
and there are many who can wait
no longer.
Make yourself wide as an ocean
to receive,
and in the rhythm you will flow and create...*

Chapter Fifteen

Being a Messenger

When you can hold the conception of the *one mind*—of the fact that we are all interconnected in Spirit—you are graced with the simplicity and the passageway of revealing this to others. The clothing or vehicle of the message matters not. Underneath, it all directs to one teaching, one knowing. The level of our own recognition of this is the state of grace that we have reached within ourselves. In states of grace we know, "I am here to represent love."

Words that aim to teach of "knowing" God often fall into themselves in the vastness of all that the expression of this idea must contain. The degree to which our words are heard or to which our conveyances are felt is determined by the level we are on behind those words.

Interactions emanating from Divine love will similarly defy accurate description, but our experiences *grace* in the amount of love and communion that each person can allow. We can know that each experience is deeply personal and transformative. We share from our God- experience most when we share the love that it has brought to us. As God-love graces us, we are naturally compelled…*deeply moved*…to share the love we have come to know.

There are spaces in the heart where healing and correction continually occur. These are where healing words are created in compassion. When we speak words from this place, we can know that we meet at a common place—the heart. Here, our words come out of the depths, and we feel them through our whole being. When we speak words of love on all its levels, we will create what we are saying from the depths of ourselves, from our sacred hearts.

Clarity of words is a blessing. In thoughtful speech, words project what is felt inwardly. When our lives are being lived at a simple and clear energetic level, our spoken word will represent it. We may speak less, but what we say will be concise in both meaning and depth. Our words take on a vibration as they are spoken. With positive intention added to their meaning, we are walking our talk in service to life. Only with meaningful intention can we move with our words to walk with Spirit. Similarly, words we seek out we will hear to the depth we are able to absorb.

A Simple Truth

You gift words their depth and meaning as you absorb them slowly, letting thoughts or phrases sink in gradually.

As a messenger of truth, we continue to grow in action. We must remember our Divine heritage, lovingly reminding ourselves who we are and that we are here to spread love around. God would not gift us awareness of compassionate love if we could not express it in the world. The gift of pure love through duality's veil is offered to everyone. When you are given sight, you are given the choice of your resolve. It is in the giving of yourself through love while living here that you may be an example to others, who will learn of it as they are ready to see and know.

When we hand out truth as a messenger, truth asks us to stay in Divine flow. In other words, truth says, "Keep moving with me, the love is in the giving." To live it, we must be doing. We can be living in a neighborhood, yet be worlds apart from our neighbors. To awaken a flow between us, we must go to the place where giving just happens, because giving fuels the form of love necessary to keep us all alive and thriving. Giving will always extend from the center of our hearts outward into wider and wider circles of connected hearts until, at last, spreading out country to country, planetary healing occurs.

A Simple Truth

When we see God-love in other people, we can be in a place of High reverence, for then we will have formed a level of communion with them, no matter how small.

    Reach into your heart time and time again to gift this love of which you now know to others. You are not to be attached to how this love is received, for it orders itself out perfectly. This is the highest sacrifice one could offer in service to God—the want for no-thing…but to be an open vessel for pure love flowing outward. The awareness of the eternal flame burns within, where directional flow always leads back to the center of the one truth: You need do no-thing. You only *do* then because you are called to serve this love that you are. This love is forever breathing through you, so there is no need for attachment.

    As we move higher into the energies of God and love awareness, some relationships will fall away, as one can perhaps no longer recognize the new level of vibration in truth that the other has found. Truth may always be offered out. The support of this is endless from the Spirit realm. Loving Guides and Beings from Beyond illusion's veil will offer constant support.

 The point on which many get stuck is that we can have no control over how the truth is received. It is enough to simply know that God will give you the words to speak when needed—conveying pure love eminence, a gifted action, or a willingness to help. Know that the service you give out is also a very deep teaching to yourself—perhaps the most poignant teaching to your own life. The deepest movement of ongoing growth you can make in this life is to offer this pure love out from your center, imbued with the truth of *all is one*. This is a pure level of responsibility that requires constancy to carry it forth.

 Here you are at a center point. It may draw some people to you and push others away, but the timing in the Divine current will be right for each interaction. You do not need to be concerned with results. Your deepest challenge is to stay out of your own ego's obstacles that block love expression. When you can reach that state of Being that love, know it is enough. More of this, more of that *externally*, by contrast, is never enough.

 The truest simplicity we can find is, the true, desireless state of Being and breathing love outward in God's perfection. By holding the body in a constant state of receiving Divine love flow, the self can expand to a place of balance within that allows it to be in a state of giving without depletion. The commitment that it takes to hold this balance may be misinterpreted as isolating and selfish because it requires simplifying and discernment. Still, there is unlimited potential pouring forth in flow from Spirit to your heart center. This is not a pipedream or an impossible state to sustain, but you must truly be willing in the center of your heart to receive its truth, opening to ever-deeper conscious possibilities in this life. If you are willing, this will always be unfolding in your life.

There are countless ways that your life can be lived out. How it will be is your own choice. You can choose chaos, or simplicity, or you can choose the middle ground. Know that whatever the choice, the love current will want to move through it, not under it, establishing its own rate of flow within you. You can always trust the powers of the eternal to move you along and to chart your course through experiences that cry out for love and healing. There will be correction and healing offered…and learning initiated. When situations speak of lots of emotional drama or baggage from the past, ask Spirit what your responsibility is in the situation. You will be told of your truth. Honor it in compassionate action, and then move past it. There can be no wrong in this.

As a messenger of truth in this life, a "never give up" energy is granted to you. Without the mind's dream of separation, only perfect, unwavering peace exists. You will be guided to bring it forward toward enlightenment and to help others in equal suffering. When heaven's gift of light structure makes it through to conscious awareness, it touches our ignorance with a sense of wonder. We are the miners, covering ground that many have wandered. The gems lie sleeping underfoot, awaiting our discovery through light illumination, through Spirit communing with matter. Can we make ourselves determined to be that miner on a daily basis, long after that first diamond of wonder has been found?

The energy of our life's purpose is the rainbow fire in our bellies. It is all the motivation and passion we can follow in this lifetime. When we are held in fear, out of balance or confused, the flame of purpose grows weaker within us as we struggle to channel it in clarity. In keeping our lives clearly focused toward the light of love, we will know the directives that we can choose. It is our choice to live a conscious life, or not to do so. On the conscious path, our hearts become the gateway to direct us into our creativity and purpose.

Dreams are lived out from within. We can not leave our dreams behind us because they will always follow us. Just as we think we have let them out of sight, there will be another experience to further our process of becoming. We can be gentle with ourselves, yet fluid in our approach to life, staying open to the shifts that are occurring. All dreams coming true are us recognizing who we truly are. The fullest expression of love from within is the culmination of all our dreams lived out before our eyes. In the love that we come to know we are, we let the mystery of life be our blueprint for living, for as long as we are seeking, love will work through us and fuel us ever onward in love.

Messenger Prayer

God,
Help me to remember
who I Am
and that my walking in this life,
my tasks,
are really quite manageable
to the all that I Am...Help me to remember
that I can move and expand freely
to know that in the love that I am
I will be guided....
I acknowledge that
There are no failures.
There is only learning.
Thank you for showing me
the way home
to the peace of my heart.

Om. Shalom. Amen.

*I smiled when I sensed
the fullness of my heart.
I stepped back
and saw myself wrestling with all the words.
I saw myself
just wanting to gift the love
I had been graced with.*

*"If I could just show you how," I thought.
"Put the word out and be at peace," I was told.*